Time And Transcendence

Mystical Insights Into The Jewish Calendar

Rabbi Fivish Mordechai Dalfin

In loving memory of the

Lubavitcher Rebbe

Rabbi Menachem M. Schneerson, O.B.M.

Distributed by:
Gurary Books
4701 New Utrecht Ave.
Brooklyn, N.Y. 11219
Tel: 718-437-9251
Fax: 718-437-9348

First Printing: 1996

Library of Congress Catalog Card Number: 95-092293

ISBN: 1-880880-13-X

Printed and bound in the United States

This book is dedicated

in loving memory of my dear parents

Morris D. Pataky, Moshe Ben Pinchas

and

Lilian, Brocha Bas Boruch

and my uncle

Julio, Pinchas Ben Boruch Pataky

Ernesto J. (Peretz) Pataky

In loving memory of

Selina Lukash

Pinchas A. Weberman
Rabbi, Ohev Shalom Congregation
President , Orthodox Rabbinical Council

בס''ד

פינחס אהרן ועברמאן
רב דקהל אוהב שלום מייאמי ביטש
נשיא ועד הרבנים החרדים דפלורידא

7055 Bonita Drive, Miami Beach, Florida 33141 • (305) 865-9851

Sivan, 5755 - סיון תשנ"ה

Rabbi Feivish Dalfin's book, "Time and Transcendence" is a fine addition to Judeo-English literature. It covers the twelve months of the Jewish calendar. Rabbi Dalfin based his research on the classic sacred books, including "Bnei Yisascher." Using his special style, he sets forth this important knowledge "like a set table ready to eat." Without it, the knowledge and inspiration he makes available would remain out of reach for many.

I commend him for his efforts. I commend those who will utilize his book for the enrichment of their Torah Knowledge.

ב"ה

Rabbi Yehuda Leib Schapiro

יהודא ליב שפירא

Rosh Yeshiva of Yeshiva
Gedolah of Greater Miami
And Rabbi of
Cong. Bais Menachem

2040 Alton Rd.
Miami Beach, FL 33140
(305) 531-8079

ראש ישיבה גדולה
דמיאמי רבתי
ורב ביהכ"נ בית מנחם

20 Sivan, 5755

Rabbi Faivish Dalfin is a well-known scholar in Miami, whose classes are well attended. "Time and Transcendence" will give new and deeper insights to understand the meaning of time in general, and the highlighted days of the Jewish calendar in particular.

"Time and Transcendence" enriches you with the true meaning of our holidays, thereby enhancing our enthusiasm in the celebration of our Yomim Tovim.

I wish Rabbi Dalfin much Hatzlacha and may he go "from strength to strength" in the holy work of the Rebbe, spreading Yiddishkeit and Chassidus, to ensure that we merit the coming of Moshiach speedily in our days.

Rabbi Yehuda Leib Schapiro

Boruch Hashem
6 Tishrei 5756
September30, 1995

In G-d's creation there are three basic elements - time, space and being. Each is a necessary component of our universe and whose potential needs to be actualized to fulfill its purpose in G-d's creation. It is the "being" that has the choice and capacity to imbue space and time with its proper function while utilizing all of the forces existing in these elements to serve Almighty G-d.

The founder of Chabad Chassidism Rebbe Schneur Zalman of Liadi has this lofty concept represented in his name Schnei-Or- the two illuminations - the revealed Torah and mystical Torah, need to affect and impact Lizman (rearranged letters of Zalman) time.

In this book Rabbi Faivish Dalfin has masterfully compiled and relegated many facets of our perception of time to reveal the multi layered dimensions that exit therein. For serious students of Torah and life this book makes these exotic concepts accessible, in a lucid, interesting and informative manner.

Hashem should bless your work and may it merit to be another link in the chain of revelation that will bring the revelation of Moshiach immediately fulfilling our Rebbe's O.B.M. mission and desire.

With Torah greetings and Blessings,

Sincerely,

Sholom D. Lipskar

Shul of Bal Harbour, Inc.
9500 Collins Avenue, Surfside, Florida 33154 • (305) 868-1411 • Fax (305) 861-2426
P.O. Box 6663 • Bal Harbour, Florida 33154

TABLE OF CONTENTS

Acknowledgements

With great gratitude to Hashem who constantly bestows upon us the ability to accomplish our mission in life. We must always recognize the source of our success.

One of the greatest gifts that Almighty G-d shared with us in this generation, was the impact of our revered Rebbe, Rabbi Menachem Mendel Schneerson O.B.M. The Rebbe enhanced world Jewry on all levels. The most distinguished Rabbi's, Thinkers, Philosophers, Scientists, and even the simple Jew, who just identifies as a Jew, were all touched by the warmth and sensitivity of this holy Tzadik.

I thank Hashem for the many years that I was able to absorb the teachings and guidance of the Rebbe. The Rebbe's influence on my life is all encompassing. It imbues my thought, speech, and action with a sense of Holiness and transcendence. A Yid must strive to go beyond his limitations, to break through his boundaries, and elevate his surroundings to higher levels of spirituality.

There is a saying that you don't write a book, you're always rewriting. This process is similar to building a edifice. Our Rabbis tell us that Letters are like stones. When you combine several letters you form a word, just as you build a foundation for a house from many stones together. It was very difficult to "build" the foundation and structure for this book. I began searching for the proper material and gather my team of friends who helped me bring this to fruition.

I started collecting my thoughts for this book two years ago on my trip to meet many Jewish inmates throughout the country on behalf of the Aleph Institute. I was sitting in back of the plane writing the first chapter which was later edited numerous times. Our Rabbis tell us that one mitzvah brings another mitzvah. The reward for impacting Jews in prison is the formation of these writings.

My deepest love goes to my wife Chaya Sara, who stood by my side and inspired me. She maintained the order at home, spending time with our children and educating them, while I spent many hours away, working on my book.

I hope and pray that my children, Mendy, Yossi, Shlomie and Chani, will grow-up with the appreciation for Torah and Mitzvahs and will continue the legacy of our ancestors, to serve Hashem with joy.

My dear grandparents Hinda Fraida Bas Reb Asher Anshel Ha'Cohen O.B.M. and Shlomo Menashe and my grandparents Shlomo and Bela Dalfin O.B.M. who survived the Holocaust and remained steadfast in their commitment to Yiddishkeit. My grandmother Hinda Fraida taught me to be a proud and strong Jew. My grandfather Shlomo had a passion for studying Torah.

My wonderful parents Reb Aaron Hillel and Miriam Dalfin who nurtured me and provided the best education. They showed me the pageantry of Judaism and the notion of being content with my portion in life.

My dear in-laws Reb Meir and Tzipora Harlig for their wonderful moral support and their Chassidishe ambiance.

My brothers Rabbi Chaim Dalfin and Anshel Dalfin and my sister Rochel Sheindel, may Hashem bless them and their families with an abundance of health, nachas and parnasa.

I would like to thank my dear friends Nathan Lederman who contributed with the artwork and Terence Speyer who spent countless hours bringing this project to reality and enhancing the beauty by editing, designing the cover, typesetting/layout, and artwork. Without Terry's assistance and insight it would be impossible for me to accomplish this task. May Hashem bless them right away with strength, health, nachas and prosperity.

I would also like to acknowledge Joel and Ira Sussman for their input and encouragement as well as Michael Chesal and Rabbi Michael Lozenik for their advice.

A special thank-you to Rabbi Sholom Dov-Ber Lipskar who works so diligently to perpetuate the forces of Yiddishkeit and is always moving forward with the Rebbe's message.

A very special appreciation to all of you who contributed to underwrite some the costs of this book. It is in your merit that many Jews will learn Torah and explore deeper dimensions of their Jewishness. May Hashem bless all of you and your families.

Amen.

PREFACE

Why devote this book to an analysis of the Jewish calendar and the meaning of colors?

Why is the creation of the Jewish calendar the first Mitzvah?

The Torah reveals the answers to all of our questions.

The Torah tells us that the first *Mitzvah* that Hashem commanded the Jewish people to perform, via Moshe, was: *Hachodesh Hazeh Lochem Rosh Chodoshim*, "This month (Nissan) shall be the head of all the months." Since this is the first *Mitzvah*, within it is reflected all of the *Mitzvahs*. Hashem commanded that the first month is the "Month of Redemption." Nissan by definition contains the essence of Hashem, which is revealed through the process of redemption.

The Jewish calendar is based on the lunar cycle. As it says in The Midrash, "the Jewish people are compared to the moon." Just as the moon receives its light from the sun, the Jewish people receive their spiritual light from Hashem's words in the Torah. Just as the moon evolves physically throughout the month, at times it is brighter than other times, so too have the Jewish people gone through tremendous turmoil throughout history and still serve G-d with joy. Just as the moon illuminates the darkness, the Jewish people maintain their faith and hope in Hashem even during the darkest moments of exile.

The creation of the calendar illustrates the fundamentals of Judaism; to be humble by recognizing that we originate from a higher source, to accept and act upon G-d's words, to have an unwavering faith in Hashem and to hope and pray for our ultimate redemption which is imminent.

The first word in the portion of the creation of the Jewish calendar is "Hachodesh" meaning *the month*. The word "Chodesh" also has another interpretation "Chidush" meaning *renewal/nuance*. The cycle of the moon is renewed each month as opposed to the cycle of the sun which is annual. The idea of renewal is fundamental to Judaism. We find in the "Shema" the verse "*these words which I command you today*," and as Rashi explains that a Jew must renew his enthusiasm to serve Hashem, as if the Torah was given today.

How does a Jew reach such a commitment in his service to Hashem?

This is explained in the concept of "Yitzias Mitzrayim," the exodus from Egypt which was told to Moses immediately after the laws pertaining to the Jewish calendar. The root of the word "Mitzrayim" is "Meitzar" meaning constraints and limitations. A Jew must transcend his limitations by connecting with the essence of Hashem. This is the process of redemption which is experienced on many levels both spiritually and physically.

The creation of the calendar which encompasses "*Time*" is in close proximity to the idea of "*Transcendence*," reveals to us the objective of a Jew in this world. *To imbue the world with the holy forces of G-dliness. To elevate the mundane elements of physicality to the highest realms of spirituality.*

This concept is reflected in the deeper meaning of colors. Colors signify the different types of energies that Hashem reveals to the physical world. The Tabernacle (Holy abode of Hashem) was decorated with a collage of colors that beautified the Temple. Colors are a reflection of Hashem's glory, which is a manifestation of His essence. The purpose of the Beis Hamikdash was to elevate materialism to a higher cause. This was enhanced through the pageantry of the Temple. When a Jew entered into the Temple he experienced the fusion of physicality and spirituality by witnessing the awesomeness of Almighty G-d's presence, breaking through all the barriers of concealments found in the physical world. In this holy environment a Jew was able to recognize that beauty and materialism were only created for a higher purpose, to enable us to see the greatness and infinite power of Hashem.

This concept is relevant to every Mitzvah. The Talmud tells us that we should beautify the Mitzvahs. Therefore a person should try to purchase a good quality Teffilin and Mezzuzah, even if they are expensive. However the main "beauty" should be from within us, and not to focus on the externalities. The Mitzvahs should be performed with emotions and feelings, it must come from our heart. This is the true honor that we give to Hashem. The purpose of creation is for

Hashem to have a dwelling place in this physical and coarse world. Each time a Jew studies Torah and performs a Mitzvah he reveals the essence of Hashem in the lowest levels. "Colors" therefore symbolize the joy and happiness that a Jew derives from his service to Hashem. This prepares the world for the ultimate revelation of Hashem through Moshiach, when the entire world will recognize the sovereignty of Almighty G-d.

Our Rabbis tell us that there is a connection between the twelve months and the twelve tribes. Hashem laid the foundation for future generations with the formation of the twelve tribes. These were the sons of Jacob who ensured that our traditions were maintained in Egypt. They are the foundation of the Jewish people and represent a higher level of knowledge.

We find in the Torah that Jacob blessed his children, each tribe according to its unique mission in the world. The land of Israel was divided into twelve sections, each tribe having its own territory. The essential connection among all of the Jewish people united them to be an everlasting nation.

What is the essential connection that binds us together?

Hashem is that connection. Through the Torah we are able to experience the oneness of Hashem. Understanding the Torah's perspective of each month, gives us insight into the significance of each month and a better understanding of our history and roots. It clarifies and refines us, so that we become aware of our objectives and of the fundamentals which enable us to relate to our Jewishness. When a Jew explores these concepts, he becomes enlightened and yearns to explore the new dimensions of Torah that have yet to be revealed. He starts to recognize the "neshoma" and its powers. This knowledge enhances his connection with G-d as well as his relationships with other people.

There is an undeniable sense of continuity to the Jewish calendar. Each month escorts us into the next month with a sense of spiritual guidance and historical connection. Jewish life revolves around the holidays. They permeate the Jew with a sense of identity. Each holiday becomes a link in the chain, an essential ingredient in a systematic progression designed by Hashem. Even the months that lack holidays have special events that remind us of who we are and what we must do.

The effect of this enhanced awareness, on a practical level, is to enable us to make informed decisions. When we understand the essence of who we are, we become more conscious of our role in life. This new focus reveals an essential truth; everything has a prescribed purpose. Studying the esoteric parts of Torah reveals the essence of the Jew.

This text is geared towards a mystical interpretation. An understanding of Jewish mysticism exposes the deeper dimensions of life and Torah. Deeper channels are opened and the hidden aspects of Torah are more revealed. We become enlightened as to how profound each seemingly simple element is.

If a Hebrew letter is so important, what about a word? The person uttering the word? Nothing is trivial.

Every Jew has to impact his community in his or her unique manner. If writing a book will help someone untangle the web of confusion, then I have somewhat accomplished my goal of bringing to life the well-springs of Torah. Especially after the sad day of Gimmel Tamuz, the passing of the Lubavitcher Rebbe the world has become darker spiritually and we feel the pressure of Golus (exile) more severely. We must increase in Torah, which is light, to counterbalance the negativity. I have the great honor and privilege to quote and explain throughout the book the holy thoughts of our revered Rebbe, O.B.M, numerous times. The Rebbe's teachings encompass all aspects of Torah from the abstract of Kabbalah to the practical directives of a Jews behavior.

I will also quote from the writings of respected Chassidic leaders and followers of the Chabad philosophy. Chassidus provides a deep and profound insight into the concept of Moshiach, the basis of Judaism. When all Jews accept this truth, G-d's presence will be revealed. All elements of Judaism are integrated. Everything branches off from the essence; the concept of Moshiach. An insight into a mystical interpretation of Torah rewards each and every Jew, no matter how extensive his religious education, with an awareness of how these spiritual and historical experiences affect contemporary life.

Let us hope and pray that through my small contribution to the study of Torah, Hashem will bless the entire community of Israel immediately with an abundance of health, happiness, peace of mind, prosperity, peace throughout the world, through the coming of Moshiach now!

Rabbi Feivish Mordechai Dalfin
Rosh Chodesh Kislev 5756
Surfside, Florida

Introduction

Each month of the Jewish calendar represents a unique manifestation of G-dliness. This is revealed throughout each month on several levels. The Sefer Yetzirah, The Book of Formation attributed to Avraham Avinu (our father Abraham), discusses the unique qualities of each month. Every month possesses a specific mission assigned by Hashem at the beginning of time.

The Likutei Hashas, a collection of the teachings of Rabbi Yitzchok Luria (16th. century), in which he details his version of the Sefer Yetzirah, describes the connection between the twelve months of the year and the twelve tribes of Israel. Rabbi Luria, also known as the Arizal, also assigned to each month a letter from the Hebrew alphabet and a defining personal characteristic.

Rabbi Tzvi Eli Melech M'Dinuv, a holy Tzadik (19th. century), in his supreme wisdom, wrote the book: B'Nai Yisaschar. He profoundly explains, in great detail, the singular nature of each month in our calendar. This book has been embraced by Jews worldwide since it was published in the last century. Its impact continues to this day.

This concept is reflected in both the name of the month and its numerical value. The names of the twelve months indicate the specific mission of each period which, in turn, corresponds to its associated tribe. Finally, the letter of the month integrates all of these holy notions.

Our Rabbi's tell us that the names of the months were brought back with the Jews from Babylonian exile (Iraq). However in mystical sources it is revealed that the origin of these names were transmitted to Moses from G-d as part of the Oral Torah. These names, which are not enumerated in the five books of Moses, became the common language of the people, because of the darkness of exile we needed an infusion of light. These names activated the inner forces of these months, and clarified the mission of each month as shown in this book.

We also find in mystical writings that the leap year (the extra month is connected with the tribe of Levi) which contains 13 months, corresponds to the 13 attributes of G-d's mercy. Every element in creation has a source in Torah. The reason why there are 12 months during the year is because they are linked with the 12 tribes. The whole purpose of creation was for the Jewish people and Torah. Therefore the numbers that are significant in Torah and the Jewish people have an impact and are reflected in the natural process of time and space.

According to the Sefer Mishnas Chasidim, by Rabbi Emanuel Chai, a sacred book of Kaballah based on the Zohar and the writings of the Arizal, each month possesses a Posuk, a verse in the Torah which represents this period. Each verse contains G-d's ineffable name in a different way. These holy letters are the channels through which Hashem's blessings for the month flow. The unique mission assigned to each month of our calendar is reflected in its Posuk. Torah, the conduit for Hashem's energy, specifies the objective of each month.

Hashem instructed the twelve tribes to carry Degalim, banners, when they traveled through the desert. Each flag had a unique color which matched the hue of one of the twelve precious gems found on the breastplate of the Kohen Gadol. The colors of these banners reveal the magnitude of each tribe's mission. Every banner also displayed the symbol of each tribe's special merit. The exquisite colors of these flags reflected the Jews' commitment to Hashem, which brought forth great love from the Almighty.

An essential element to comprehending the meaning of each month is an understanding of its relationship to its numerical value. In Hebrew, every letter of the alphabet equals a specific number. G-d Almighty created the world with His holy tongue, the Hebrew alphabet. These letters are the channels through which Hashem's energy is manifested in the physical world. Each letter reveals a different form of energy. The numerical value of each letter conveys another dimension of this process.

The Sefer Yetzirah declares that during each month we must concentrate on a specific character trait. We have to modify our behavior in order to achieve a higher level of sensitivity. The Torah emphasizes the importance of action. We are not permitted to learn only abstract concepts, we must implement the words of G-d into our daily lives. By refining our conduct we find ourselves closer to the Almighty.

Introduction II - The True Meaning of Colors

The Torah discusses colors in a number of places, three of them are explained here.

I. The Rainbow. As we know, God promised to Noah that He will never flood the world again. However, there are times when the world is in such a state of spiritual decline, that Hashem would like to punish the world. The rainbow is a sign that God's anger has been provoked. There is a law that one should not stare at the rainbow. You may look briefly and recite a blessing.

II. The Mishkan. The material used for the coverings of the Tabernacle was a mixture of many colors of threads. (Parsha Trumah 26:31)

III. The clothing and breastplate of the Cohen Gadol. (Tetzava 28:5, 17-20). The garments were woven in a skilled fashion which combined a multitude of colorful threads. The breastplate worn by the High Priest had 12 stones, each of a different color. Each color represented one of the twelve tribes.

Kaballah gives us a deeper insight into the significance of colors, in connection with the attributes of Hashem. Almighty G-d reveals himself in many different ways, displaying kindness, severity, compassion, victory, splendor, foundation and sovereignty. We see that the energy in the world is a reflection of G-d's manifestation. G-d reveals himself through many different channels. These channels correspond to different colors: white, black, red, blue, green, gold, and a mixture of all of them. For example, a lighter color such as white, represents G-d's kindness. A darker color, on the other hand, symbolizes G-d's severity. A mixture of colors (if it is leaning towards a lighter color) sometimes represents G-d's compassion. In order for the colors to be displayed, there must be light. G-d, of course, is the source of light. The mechanism of creation was light.

Why was there such emphasis on the beauty of colors in the construction of the Mishkan? The holy Temple was the abode for G-d's presence where He revealed himself. The physical beauty was a manifestation of the spiritual pageantry. The light that imbued all the colors was the infinite light of G-dliness. The twelve stones on the breastplate of the Cohen gadol reflected the holy levels of spirituality attained by each of the twelve tribes.

Now, the colors of the rainbow are dull/faded. In the holy Zohar it is written that we will see the bright flashy colors of the rainbow, and this will be a sign of the imminence of Moshiach. When Moshiach comes, the world will be imbued with the knowledge of God which will in turn bring out the splendor of creation. It is written that Torah is light, and when a Jew studies Torah, the world is illuminated with the multi-colored infinite light of Hashem.

Introduction III
The Fundamental Teachings of the Baal Shem Tov

In order to have a better understanding of the concepts discussed in this book, we need some insight into the foundation of the teachings of Chassidus. As we know, the holy Tzaddik, Reb Yisroel Baal Shem Tov (18 Elul 1698 - Shavuos 1760) was the founder of the Chassidic movement. He emphasized three principles of the Torah.

I. Divine Providence. To see and to feel that everything that occurs in a Jew's life is an act of God and to have full faith that Hashem is constantly with us. This security gives us the tranquility necessary for a Jew even in the most difficult times.

II. The Baal Shem Tov taught that we are to embrace every single Jew. Even the most simple Jews are to be treated with the same dignity and respect as the greatest Rabbis. The Jewish people united together are likened to the human body. Just as the head plays a vital role in the well being of the individual, nevertheless it still needs the legs to fully function in its proper capacity. Similarly, the leaders need to be united with the general population. In fact, he said that the mitzvahs of the simple Jew "touches" the essence of Hashem which is sometimes lacking by the scholar.

III. To serve Hashem with Joy. It is not sufficient just to perform the mitzvahs. It must be imbued with enthusiasm of the heart and soul.

These three ideas are integrated with each other. When a Jew believes that everything is by divine providence he becomes sensitive even to the most trivial occurances. He realizes that there is holy energy in every part of creation. This raises him to a higher spiritual level and brings him closer to every Jew, knowing that the other Jew has a G-dly soul just as he does. When a person has this awareness and sensitivity he becomes content with his portion in life and serves Hashem with joy and happiness.

The Fundamental Teachings of the Founder of Chabad Chassidism Rabbi Shneuer Zalman of Liadi — The Alter Rebbe

I. Chabad. In addition to the teachings of the Baal Shem Tov, the Alter Rebbe (18 Elul 1745 - 24 Teves 1812) emphasized that it is necessary to internalize the beliefs and teachings of Torah in our intellect. The word Chabad is an acronym of three words: Chochma-wisdom, Binah-understanding, and Das-knowledge. Almighty God has blessed all of us with the capacity of intelligence. We must utilize our talents to their fullest measure. One's belief in God must penetrate the deepest levels of the mind in order for the mind to become a vehicle for Hashem's presence. When a Jew immerses himself in the study of Torah and understands its brilliance, Almighty God then embraces him with a total unification of the individual's mind with Hashem and Torah.

II. Service of Davening. Prayer is not only to beseech Hashem for our needs. Tefillah, the Hebrew word for prayer, literally means "connection." When a Jew connects with Hashem it refines and sensitizes him. Davening is the service of the heart. Before one begins to daven, he must contemplate on the awesomeness of Almighty God. This concentration is developed through learning Chassidus prior to davening. Many Chassidim would daven for many hours for the purpose of experiencing and enhancing their relationship with Hashem.

III. Teshuva — the Hebrew word for Repentance or Return. Every Jew has the responsibility for cleansing and elevating his soul. Teshuva is not only an act of remorse for transgressions, it also means to "return." This concept of "return" denotes moving closer to Hashem by elevating yourself spiritually through constant growth in Torah and mitzvos. Thus, even a Tzaddik, a righteous person, must constantly reach for a higher level.

The Fundamental Teachings of the Rebbe
Rabbi Menachem Mendel Schneerson

I. Ahavas Yisroel - Love for a Fellow Jew. The Rebbe (11 Nissan 5662/1902 - 3 Tammuz 5754/1994) stressed that love for a fellow Jew requires Mesiras Nefesh, self-sacrifice. This love encompasses both the spiritual and physical well being of the recipient. We must be consumed with the urgency of assisting each and every Jew.

II. To Disseminate the Wellsprings of Chassidus. The teachings of Chassidus is critical to world Jewry. It awakens the deepest levels of the Neshama, the G-dly soul, and focuses our attention to the priorities of Torah and Mitzvos.

III. To alert World Jewry with the need for Torah education. When you imbue a child with an awareness of Hashem you lay the foundation for Jewish continuity. Without a proper education he is vulnerable to outside influences which leads him in the wrong direction. The need for education is critical for every Jew. All of us have a child inside of our Neshoma, which is hungry and thirsty for Yiddishkeit.

IV. To Believe and hope for the imminence of Moshiach. The essence of Torah and Mitzvos will be revealed with the coming of Moshiach. Until then, the world is in a state of concealment. G-dliness and spirituality are obscure. A Jew must long and yearn for this great revelation.

Our Rabbis tell us that the reason for this Galus, the present exile, is baseless hatred. The Rebbe emphasized that we must express unconditional love for one another in order to atone for this transgression and bring the ultimate redemption. He also mentioned many times that we are on the threshold of Moshiach's arrival. We just have to open our eyes to see this reality.

The messianic era is similar to Shabbos. Just as a Jew is immersed with Godliness and holiness on Shabbos, this awesome feeling will be experienced for eternity with the revelation of Moshiach. One must prepare himself during the weekdays in order to enjoy the spirit of Shabbos. Similarly, we must *now* imbue our lives with the esoteric teachings of Torah in order to fully absorb the knowledge of God, which will fill the world just as the waters cover the sea.

NISSAN

Chodesh H'Aviv • Month of Redemption • The Fifteenth of Nissan - The Birth of the Jewish Nation • Exodus • The Fundamentals of Judaism • The Notion of Transcendence • The Numerical Value of the Name Nissan • The Fifty Levels of Holiness • The Tribe of Yehuda • The Color Blue on the Flag of Yehuda • The Letter Hay and Its Esoteric Meaning • The Power of Speech • The Ultimate Revelation of Moshiach

Our Fathers were redeemed from slavery in Egypt, in the merit of Emunah, because of their belief in Hashem.

-- Midrash, Yalkut Shimoni Hoshaya #519

NISSAN

Chodesh H'Aviv • Month of Redemption

The Torah[1] calls the first month of the year Chodesh H'Aviv, meaning "the month of Spring." The Rabbis[2] refer to this month as Nissan. A second name given to this month by our Rabbis[3] is "The Month of Geulah (Redemption)." The name Nissan refers to the concept of miracles. This month's connection to the notion of miracles is revealed as we observe the holiday of Pesach and celebrate the emancipation and redemption of the Jewish people.

The Fifteenth of Nissan • The Birth of the Jewish Nation

Our Rabbis[4] tell us that on Pesach, the fifteenth of Nissan, three angels visited Avraham Avinu to heal the wounds incurred during his circumcision and to tell him that Sara would give birth to a baby in a year's time. One year later, on Pesach, Yitzchak was born. On this same date[5] years later, our father Yaakov received the blessings from his father, Yitzchak. Exactly four hundred years after Yitzchak's birth, the Torah[6] declares that the Jewish people were liberated from Egyptian slavery. Seven days after the Exodus, on the twenty-first of Nissan, the Jews witnessed the splitting of the Red Sea. A year after the Exodus, on Rosh Chodesh Nissan, the Jews dedicated the Mishkan, the tabernacle, in the desert.[7]

The Exodus • The Fundamentals of Judaism

The Mitzvah of remembering Yetzias Mitzrayim, the Exodus from Egypt, is fundamental to Judaism.[8] We mention the Exodus, "Zaicher Liyitzias Mitzrayim," at Friday night Kiddush and on holidays. We recall this event in our daily recitation of the Shema which concludes with the Mitzvah of remembering the Exodus. It is essential for Jewish men to think of the great wonders of Yetzias Mitzrayim as they fulfill the Mitzvah of Tefillin. Why is the precept of Yetzias Mitzrayim so fundamental? The answer lies within the word Mitzrayim.

The Hebrew word for Egypt, Mitzrayim, is a combination of, Metzar and Yam, meaning "narrow" and "sea." Both words allude to the notion of obscuring reality. Bodies of water conceal all that they contain. The term narrow is often used to refer to constraints. For example, a person who is narrow-minded is limited and does not see with a sense of clarity.[9]

A person who only seeks worldly goals conceals the truth of Hashem's power. The Hebrew word for world is Olom, which resembles to Helm, meaning concealment. We exist in a state of darkness and confusion. It may seem as if the world operates according to laws prescribed by nature. In reality it is Almighty G-d who is in control. It is Hashem who constantly creates and coordinates the natural world. Hashem hides and cloaks Himself within nature. Nothing is random. For example, we do not expect to experience heat during the winter months. The act of concealing G-dliness is demonstrated through the word Mitzrayim.

The Notion of Transcendence

Each Jew must transcend his limitations and connect with the Torah in order to experience the Exodus of his own Mitzrayim.[10] We must release ourselves from the Yetzer Hara, the evil animalistic impulse, to become free. When we liberate ourselves from the bondage of emotions, monetary concerns, and lust, we are free to ascend to higher levels. When a Jew performs a Mitzvah or studies Torah, he connects with Hashem, the source of everything. He then ascends and elevates all that surrounds him to holier heights. The objective of Judaism is to release us from our personal constraints and connect with the essence of Hashem.

The culmination of the Exodus was Krias Yam Suf, the splitting of the Red Sea. Almighty G-d had many methods through which he could have rescued the Jews from the Egyptian onslaught. He chose to divide the sea. The division of the waters is a metaphor for the revelation of the Truth. This experience was required prior to the revelation of the Ten Commandments. A Jew must remove all which conceals G-dliness in order to experience the reality of Hashem's being.[11]

Every day we are commanded to remember the historical events surrounding the Exodus. We relive this holy experience and emerge spiritually revitalized. When a Jew bursts forth from his bonds, his personal Mitzrayim, he can see the reality of Almighty G-d. After witnessing the splitting of the sea and revealing the wondrous energy beneath the murky waters, each Jew can proceed to the next holy experience on his journey to receive the Torah. Each day Hashem gives us an additional revelation of Torah. In order to receive this gift we must continue to experience Yetzias Mitzrayim.

Another example of transcendence is the act of circumcision. Avraham circumcised himself at age 99,[12] and Yitzchak was born to Avraham when he was 100 years old and Sara was 90 years of age. Both of these events occurred during Nissan and reveal miracles transcending the laws of nature. The act of circumcision at such an advanced age is an act of transcendence, since Avraham ignored his physical pain in order to fulfill G-d's commandments. The birth of the first Jewish child, Yitzchak, was also a miracle. This wondrous event set in motion the legacy of the Jewish people, imbuing us with a future based upon miracles. Our survival throughout history is a miracle within itself.

The dedication of the Mishkan (sanctuary) on Rosh Chodesh Nissan, emphasizes the notion of transcendence. On this day, the Torah states [13] that a flame descended upon the altar from heaven. This powerful revelation was the confirmation of Almighty G-d's presence in the physical world. Hashem permanently imbued physicality with His holiness. This experience assured the Jewish people that G-d had forgiven the transgression of the Golden Calf.

The name of the month, Aviv, means "spring." However, upon analysis we note a more profound message. Aviv is the combination of Av and Yud-Bais, meaning a "father to twelve." This month leads all twelve months of the calendar. A second interpretation deems that Av, refers to Hashem, our Father, who had mercy on the twelve tribes of Israel.[14]
The numerical value of Aviv is 15. This refers to the fifteenth of the month, the day our people left the bonds of Egypt. Av equals 3. This refers to our three forefathers, Avraham, Yitzchak, and Yaakov. It was in their merit that our people were emancipated from slavery in Mitzrayim. Yud-Bais equals twelve, a reference to the twelve tribes of Israel.

The Fifty Levels of Holiness

The name Nissan begins with the letter Nun, which has a numerical value of 50. Our sages[15] tell us that there are 50 Levels of Holiness. It is imperative also to recognize that parallel to this notion of purity there exists a corresponding 50 levels of unholiness and impurity. In Egypt, prior to the Exodus, the Jewish people fell to the 49th level of contamination. Consequently, it was necessary for Hashem to sanctify them with righteousness derived from the 50 Gates of Holiness, saving the Jews from sinking to the fiftieth level of impurity, thereby hastening their liberation.[16]

The Talmud[17] tells us that the letter Nun refers to the word Nifilah, meaning "falling." This first letter in the name Nissan is the letter which points to the profane manner in which the Jews lived while enslaved in Egypt. On the other hand, the Talmud[18] says that the final letter of Nissan, also a Nun, refers to Nissim Nissim, which translates to "a multiple of miracles."

The Numerical Value of the Name Nissan

The numerical sum of Nissan is 170, or twice 85. Eighty-five is the numerical value of the word "Peh," meaning mouth. The word Nissan, therefore, translates to "two times mouth." The first allegorical reference to the mouth of G-d, the source of expression and revelation, is a reference to verbal communication; speech reveals what was concealed within our private thoughts. This alludes to the revelation of Almighty G-d Himself which lead to the birth of the Jewish identity during the Exodus from Egypt. The second reference to "mouth" foreshadows the imminent wonders yet to come, when Moshiach is revealed and G-dliness will saturate the world like water fills the ocean. [19]

This concept is expressed in the word Pesach. Pesach is a combination of Peh and Sach, meaning "a mouth that speaks," alluding to the wondrous revelation of Hashem during the Exodus.[20]

Spiritual Circumcision

The word traditionally associated with the numerical value 85 is Milah, meaning "circumcision." Rashi tells us[21] that before the Jews were taken out of Egypt, Hashem required that they all be circumcised in order to be worthy of the Exodus, just as Avraham and Yitzchak had experienced the Mitzvah of Milah during this month many years before. The concept of circumcision refers, once again, to the notion of revelation of G-d, which took place at the time of the Exodus. Through this physical procedure, the foreskin is removed and the genuine nature of the organ can be seen. Spiritually, circumcision refers to the removal of the decay which hides the Neshoma. As Nissan equals twice 85, there is a higher level of circumcision which we will experience with the imminent revelation of Moshiach. As it is written in the Torah: "G-d will circumcise the foreskin of our hearts." With the arrival of Moshiach, Hashem will sensitize us to feel the powerful values of Torah and Mitzvahs.

The Tribe of Yehuda

The tribe of Yehuda is associated with the month of Nissan. Both Nissan's primary position in the Jewish calendar and its relationship to the tribe of Yehuda highlight the sovereignty of Hashem, the fundamental principle of Judaism that we reaffirm in all of our prayers. As the Jewish people accepted Hashem's monarchy and expressed uncompromising faith in Him by leaving their homes and embarking on a journey of uncertainty, Hashem liberated them from slavery to Pharaoh and they became servants to the King of all Kings.

This concept of leadership is reflected in the life of the original Yehuda, the son of Yaakov. The Torah [22] states that Yehuda was chosen to be the king of the Jewish nation personifying authority, royalty, and dignity. He convinced his brothers not to kill Yosef as a punishment for causing dissension within the family. Yehuda also had the strength and courage to admit publicly that he had begotten children with Tamar, his son's widow, even though it caused him great embarrassment.[23]

The name of the tribe Yehuda is derived from "Hapam Oideh Es Hashem," meaning "this time I thank Hashem."[24] Each Jew is referred to as a Yehudi.[25] The reason is because every Jew innately thanks Hashem as a result of his belief in the Almighty. In the name Yehuda, we find the four letters of G-d's name, Yud - Kay - Vov - Kay, and an additional Dalet.[26] The Dalet in Hebrew means poverty and humility. We can, therefore, see that by humbling ourselves before Hashem, the true nature of a Jew is revealed. Yehuda teaches us to accept the sovereignty of G-d with full faith, by assuming a leadership position and by taking no individual pride in our mission. Therefore, the month of Nissan is the first month because the initial step of a Jew is to accept G-d's sovereignty,[27] this is reflected in the theme of Nissan as well as the tribe of Yehuda.

The Color Blue

The flag of Yehuda is blue with an embroidered lion.[28] Both the color and the emblem reflect the tribe's royal status. The Talmud[29] tells us that the color blue suggests the sky which is a reflection of G-d's throne of glory. Yehuda is the earthly personification of the majesty of Hashem. The lion is the king of the beasts. Yaakov, in his blessings to Yehuda, compares him to a lion.

We also find the concept of the acceptance of G-d's sovereignty during the Exodus related directly to the tribe of Yehuda. They were the first to demonstrate leadership in acceptance of G-d's kingship. The tribe of Yehuda revealed courage through their actions when the Jews fled Egypt and were stopped at the Red Sea. The leader of the tribe of Yehuda, Nachshon ben Aminadav, and his tribe, jumped into the Red Sea rather than surrender to the pursuing Egyptians.[30] Their faith in Hashem resulted in the parting of the waters so all of the Jews could escape. Therefore, Yehuda was chosen to be the tribe from which the kings of Israel would come forth. King David and King Solomon are descendants of Yehuda. Ultimately, Moshiach's lineage will be traced to this tribe, chosen by Hashem to be the source of royalty.[31]

The Letter Hay and Its Esoteric Meaning

Hashem created the Hebrew language and the Almighty manifests Himself through its letters.[32] The Hebrew letter Hay, which the Arizal associates with the month of Nissan, first appears as a "word" in the Torah[33] when Yosef was the viceroy in Egypt and the land fell victim to a famine. The people came to Yosef, their leader, pleading for food and he replied: "HAY Lachem Zera" meaning "here is to you seed." Once again, we find a connection to the concept of sovereignty. Yosef was in a position to dispense food, the source of life, and his people deferred to his decree. The appearance of the letter HAY in relationship to the concept of "life," (Yosef dispensing seed), will be explained further.

The letter Hay also assumes a prominent role in the story of Avraham. Avram became Avraham after his circumcision.[34] The Almighty added the Hay to Avram's name in order to signify our forefather's acceptance of Hashem's sovereignty. This story also reiterates the connection between the Hebrew words Peh and Milah, "mouth" and "circumcision," and extends the relationship to include the letter Hay and the authority of G-d.

What is the connection between the letter Hay and the notion of kingship? The qualities of the letter Hay are reflected in its pronunciation. It is produced solely with an exhalation of breath. All other letters of the Hebrew alphabet transform our breaths into their individual sounds. Therefore, the letter Hay, being the phonetic source of all other letters, reminds us of Hashem's position as the source of all life. Just as a king governs through his words, so does the King of all Kings rule through his G-dly language.[35]

The transformation of G-d's breath into letters reminds us of the evolution of breath into life. The Torah[36] tells us, Hashem "blew" the breath of life into Adam. A Jew is born when Hashem breathes life into him. The Neshoma, or "soul," emanates from Hashem, the source. The Jewish people were "born" during the month of Nissan.[37] When they were circumcised prior to leaving Egypt they received the gift of their Neshoma, or "soul." Hay is the root of all other letters; the beginning, just as Nissan is the beginning of the year.

The Power of Speech

The Arizal associates the characteristic of speech with the month of Nissan, the tribe of Yehuda, and the letter Hay. Speech should be used only to exalt Hashem.[38] A Jew must direct his energy for that purpose. He should never use speech as a weapon, to slander or embarrass another person.[39] The power of life and death lies in language. By praising Hashem through prayer and the study of Torah, and by saying a kind word to our fellow Jew, our "mouth" becomes a conduit through which Hashem's energy and life force will be revealed.

The Ultimate Revelation of Moshiach

Each month of the year is identified with a specific verse in the Torah.

The month of Nissan is associated with the verse "Yismechu, (beginning with a Yud), Hashamayim, (beginning with a Hay), Visagael, (beginning with a Vav), Haaretz, (also beginning with a Hay).[40] The initial letters of these four words spell out G-d's name. This passage from one of King David's Psalms means: "The heavens should be happy and the earth should rejoice." Upon the arrival of Moshiach, all living things will recognize the sovereignty of Hashem and the power of His sustenance and wisdom. Therefore, upon the revelation of this reality, we will rejoice as we accept our true essence, the energy and power of Hashem.[41]

IYAR

Month of Ziv • Light of Torah • Mana • Spiritual Nourishment • Tzur - The Miracle of Natural Water • Amalek • Unity - The Counting of the Jews • Pesach Sheni • It Is Never Too Late • Lag B'Omer • Jewish Mysticism • Iyar G-d's Cure • The Tribe of Yisachar • The Yoke of Torah • The Ultimate Reward • Hashem's Crown • The Secrets of the Letter Vav • The Power of Thought • Knowing G-d • Hashem is the Groom and the Jews are His Bride

In the merit of the holy Zohar, we will be liberated from Golus, exile.

-- Zohar, vol. 3, p. 124B

Ziv, The Light of Torah

The second month of the Jewish year is Iyar.[1] It was during this period that the Jewish people prepared themselves with much anticipation for receiving the Torah.[2] The purpose of the Exodus was not only the creation of a defined nationality, but also to accept the holy Torah at Mt. Sinai.[3] This period is also referred to as "Ziv," meaning brightness. This is the month when we appreciate the wondrous blossoming and light of flowers.[4] The concept of light is reflected in the study of Torah. It is written[5] that Torah is compared to light.

Mana, Spiritual Nourishment

In the days following the Exodus from Egypt, the Jews found themselves without food. The Torah states[6] that on the fifteenth day of the second month, the Jews complained of hunger. Shortly thereafter, Hashem provided them with nourishment, mana from heaven. The Midrash[7] states that the Torah was given to the people who ate the mana. The consumption of the mana imbued them with holiness and refined their sensitivities. The mana that descended from heaven represents the Torah which came down from Hashem. The mana provided spiritual nourishment and produced no human waste. Torah is referred to as "food entering my stomach," the life force of every Jew.[8]

Tzur, The Miracle of Natural Water

During this month, the exiles also lacked water.[9] After informing Hashem of their discomfort, the Jews witnessed the great Miracle of the Well, "Tzur," which quenched the thirst of the entire Jewish nation. This well was not a natural spring, it was a rock which miraculously supplied fresh water. Water is essential to sustain human life just as Torah is essential to nourish every Jew's soul.

On their way to Mt. Sinai, the Jews were attacked by the nation of Amalek.[10] This enemy tried to stop the Jews on their way to receive the Torah. The Jews defeated Amalek and were instructed to erase any reference to them. Every day we encounter Amalek. As we awake each morning and prepare to Daven and learn Torah, the Yetzer Hara attempts to diminish our excitement and plays down the importance of Torah and Mitzvahs. Initially, Amalek attacks our emotions and enthusiasm towards Yiddishkeit. Eventually, this results in indifference towards a life of Mitzvahs.[11]

Unity - The Counting of the Jewish People

In *The Book of Numbers* it states that on the first day of the second month of the second year following the Exodus from Egypt, Moshe was instructed to take a census of the Jewish people. The concept of counting underscores the importance of every Jew. Each person must be counted in order to arrive at a final figure. This emphasizes Jewish unity. During the month of Iyar, we prepare for Revelation of Hashem on Shavuous. We must be united in order to receive the gift of the Torah.[12] Each year we are commanded to relive this experience so we may receive the Torah in the proper manner.

It Is Never Too Late

Another significant event that occurred during this second month of the Jewish calendar, one year after the Exodus, was Pesach Sheni.[13] When the Jews left Egypt, they carried the bones of Yosaif with them so he could be buried in Israel. The men who transported the remains were not able to bring the Pascal sacrifice. According to Jewish Law, if a person touches a dead body he becomes ritually impure. Hashem said that on the fourteenth day of the second month he would give them a second chance. This is called the day of Pesach Sheni, the Second Passover.

Even a Jew who is spiritually contaminated and alienated from a strict observance of Judaism may return to his essence through the study of Torah. This "homecoming" is demonstrated in the story of Pesach Sheni which teaches us that it is never too late. Hashem always gives us a "second chance."[14] Hashem reveals Himself in Torah, therefore, when a Jew connects with Torah he is touching the essence of G-d. Every Jew is a son of Avraham, Yitzchak, and Yaakov and our matriarchs Sara, Rivka, Rochel, and Leah who cry and pray for all of their children to return "home." It is essential for us to return to our heritage.

Another event from Jewish history, Lag B'Omer, occurred during this period.[15] This event does not appear in the Torah. It is connected, however, with the counting of the Omer, a concept that is mentioned in the scripture.[16] Jews commemorate the time that lapsed between their leaving Egypt and the day of Revelation by anxiously counting the interim 49 days, the days of the Omer, which culminate on Shavuous, the fiftieth day. Lag B' Omer falls on the thirty-third day of the Omer.

The Talmud[17] describes a tragic event which occurred between Pesach and Lag B'Omer. The great Rabbi Akivah taught 24,000 students who fell victim to a plague because they were disrespectful of each other. It was on Lag B'Omer that the dying ceased. We, therefore, commemorate this day as a joyous occasion.

Lag B'Omer • Jewish Mysticism

Rabbi Shimon bar Yochai, the great mystic and author of the holy *Zohar*, passed away on Lag B' Omer. It was his wish that people rejoice on this day.[18] To celebrate his Yahrtzeit thousands of Jews visit his burial site at Miron (Israel) each year.

Torah, contains both revealed and esoteric aspects. Rabbi Shimon bar Yochai, the master of Jewish mysticism, explored Torah's deeper dimensions. Before Shavuous, each Jew must prepare himself for the reoccurrence of the profound revelation that we experience at this time of the year. By studying Torah intensely, digesting it thoroughly, and proceeding to examine its deeper dimensions through the study of Kaballah and Chassidus, we can experience the essence of revelation during the festival of Shavuous. The study of Kaballah and Chassidus is crucial to a Jew, so that he will be able to connect the essence of his soul with the essence of G-d, and to hasten the coming of Moshiach.[19]

In *The Book of Kings*[20], it states that Shlomo Hamelech, King Solomon, began to build the Bais Hamikdash, the Holy Temple, during the month of "Ziv." The Bais Hamikdash was the physical place where Almighty G-d revealed Himself. Our Rabbis tell us that since the destruction of the Temple, Hashem reveals Himself to each Jew who studies Torah. Through the study of Torah, we become a Bais Hamikdash for the revelation of Hashem.[21]

Iyar - G-d's Cure

The name Iyar is an acronym of the words "Ani Hashem Rofecho," "I G-d am your healer,"[22] which reflects the spiritual condition of the Jewish people during the interim period between the Exodus and the Revelation. The reference to healing alludes not only to the curing of physical wounds,[23] but also to the spiritual degradation that the Jews brought with them from Egypt. This contamination had to be cleansed in order to prepare for Hashem's gift of the Torah.

Iyar is also an acronym of Avraham, Yitzchak, Yaakov, and Rochel.[24] It was in their merit that the Jews were redeemed from exile and received the gift of the Ten Commandments.[25]

The word Iyar is linked with with the word Or, meaning light. This alludes to the great light of Torah. It is in this month when we experience the "holy light," an occurrence that is commemorated on Lag B'Omer with the lighting of torches. This custom signifies the profound revelation experienced by every Jew involved in the study of Torah.[26]

The numerical value of the word Iyar is 221. (Aleph equals one, two Yuds equal twenty, and Resh is 200.) Two hundred twenty-one corresponds to the word Erech, meaning both "long" and "to heal." We find the concept of "long" in "The Thirteen Attributes of Mercy," Moshe's famous prayer which contains the following passage: "Hashem Hashem Ail Rachum Vichanun Erech Apayaim."[27] This means "Hashem is merciful and benevolent and allows *a great length of time* for us to repent for our transgressions." The second concept, that of "healing," is found in the daily prayers. We ask Hashem to cure those Jews who are ill, and we say: "Vihalay Arucha Urifuah Shlemah" meaning "We ask Hashem to bring upon us a complete cure and healing." These concepts are reflected in both the name of the month and its numerical value.

The Tribe of Yisachar • The Yoke of Torah

The tribe associated with the second month is the tribe of Yisachar.[28] Yaakov compared Yisachar to a strong-boned donkey.[29] A donkey is able to haul heavy loads. The men of Yisachar would labor day and night in their study of Torah. A donkey is dressed in a yoke when at work. Our sages[30] teach us that when a Jew accepts upon himself the yoke of Torah, Hashem removes from him the yoke of hard work. A Jew must work, but his priorities must be to serve Hashem.

This association of this tribe with the month of Iyar alludes to the theme of Torah. It is written[31] that "from the children of Yisachar there shall be great scholars." The Torah also states[32]: "Rejoice as you go out (for business) and Yisachar in your tents (of Torah)." The tribe of Yisachar devoted themselves completely to the study of Torah and became the scholars and the Rabbis of the Jewish courts.

This connection is illustrated in the flag of Yisachar. The color of the flag was dark blue, almost black. Yisachar's emblem was the sun and moon.[33] This dark cast is a classical example of humility, it lacks the arrogance of a flashy color. This echoes a fundamental lesson of Torah; to be humble before G-d. The depiction of the sun and moon indicates that the Rabbis from this tribe were knowledgeable in astronomy, and were, therefore, able to form the Jewish calendar. Through the study of Torah they touched the glory of Hashem and were inspired by his majesty.

In the Torah,[34] we find the word Yisachar spelled as Yisaschar. It is, however, pronounced Yisachar. Yisachar is the personification of Torah. The Torah contains revealed concepts and those which are concealed, the secret and mystical aspects. When we don't pronounce the second Shin in the word Yisachar we allude to the hidden aspects of Torah.[35]

The Ultimate Reward • Hashem's Crown

If the correct spelling was to be divided phonetically, we would find the words Yesh and Sachar, meaning "there is a reward." The numerical value of the word Yesh is 310. When you study Torah you are rewarded with the revelation of 310 levels of G-dliness. As it says in the conclusion of the Mishnah:[36] "In the world to come, every Tzadik will inherit 310 worlds." The numerical equivalent of Kesser, crown, is 620. Three hundred and ten is exactly half of 620. The higher level of the "crown," the first 310 levels, is revealed to those who participate in the study of Torah. The higher level of the "crown," represented by 310, is the essence of G-d which is beyond revelation. Hashem and his children, the Jewish people, are one entity with Almighty G-d. Therefore, the Mishnah explains that the inheritance of every Tzadik will be the personal experience of these 310 levels of G-dliness which are manifested in Hashem's crown.[37]

The numerical value of the word Yisaschar is 830. Yud equals 10, two Shins equal 600, Chaf equals 20, and Resh equals 200. Eight hundred and thirty is the precise number of years that the two Temples, the Bais Hamikdash, stood in Yerushalayim. As we stated, the word Yisaschar can be phonetically divided as Yesh Sachar, "there is reward." This alludes to the great reward given in recognition for the study of Torah that was experienced with the two Temples, where we saw and felt G-dliness.

During the month of Iyar, the Jewish people prepared for the giving of the Torah. As the Jews still functioned on a low level of holiness, they needed an incentive to maintain the positive momentum of the Exodus which was to culminate in the acceptance of Hashem's gift of the Torah. Therefore, Hashem promised them great reward for their acceptance of His holy Torah.

The Secrets of the Letter Vav

The Arizal tells us that the month of Iyar is associated with the letter Vav.[38] In the sacred Zohar, it is written that the letter Vav personifies Emes, "the absolute truth."[39] This refers to the Torah which is called Toras Emes. According to Hebrew grammar, Vav is a conjunction, many times connecting concepts which appear to be opposing. We find the word Vav mentioned in the Torah when Hashem details the construction of the tabernacles in the desert.[40] The word Vav means "a hook," used to connect the cloth coverings of the sanctuary. The concept of connection illustrated by the Vav/hook demonstrates the essential connection of every single Jew to Hashem through Torah, the spiritual hook. The profundity of this sense of connection is clear. The sanctuary is the place where our essential bond to Hashem is revealed. It is from the sanctuary that we get inspiration throughout our daily affairs. Even a Jew who appears to oppose a strict observance of Judaism is connected to his essence just as the Vav links together opposing concepts.

The Power of Thought

The Arizal tells us that the personal characteristic emphasized during the month of Iyar is "deep thought." This teaches us that a Jew must study Torah not only on a superficial level, but also to immerse himself completely in his study. It is written,[41] "With all my bones I will praise you." As it is explained in the holy *Zohar*, the reason that we "shuckle and sway" when we study Torah and when we pray is because the soul is compared to the flame of a candle. Just as the flame never stands still so too the G-dly soul vibrates when it connects with Hashem through Torah and prayer.[42]

Knowing G-d

The verse in the Torah which corresponds to the month of Iyar is "Yis-haleil Hamis-haleil Haskeil Viyodayah."[43] The initial four letters of these words, when rearranged, spell out G-d's name. The translation of this verse is: "The one who praises shall praise and use his intellect to know G-d." Once again, we see how this illustrates the theme of the month, the intense study of Torah, and ultimately, knowing (connecting with) G-d. As it is written:[44] "And Adam knew Eve." The verb "to know" is often used to indicate intimacy, a form of connection. When the Torah refers to the relationship between the Jewish people and Hashem at the time of revelation, Hashem is often called the "groom" and the Jews are the "bride."[45] Through the study of Torah, we unite in a symbolic marriage with G-d and become one with Him. This experience will be magnified in the near future with the revelation of Hashem through Moshiach.

SIVAN

Revelation • The Warmth of Torah • To See G-d • Sin/Sinai • Sivan and Kislev • Torah Illuminates the Darkest Corners of the World • Humility: The Vessel for G-dliness • Blueprint of Creation • Emes - Eternity • The Tribe of Zevulun • The Importance of Supporting Torah Study • The Emblem of the Ship • The Mission of the Soul • The Power of the Letter Zayin • The True Meaning of Walking • To Construct an Abode for Hashem

Hashem studies alongside each Jew who learns Torah.

-- Midrash, Tana Dvei Eliyahu, ch. 18

SIVAN

Revelation

The name of the third month is Sivan.[1] The highlight of this month is the revelation of Hashem to the Jewish people on the sixth day of Sivan. The Torah describes at length, the great excitement that took place at Mt. Sinai before and during the Revelation.[2]

The Warmth of Torah

There are two opinions amongst Jewish scholars as to the translation of the name Sivan. Sivan is spelled Samech, Yud, Vav, Nun. Since the Hebrew letters Zayin and Samech are interchangeable, the pronunciation could be interpreted as Zivan, meaning the "ray and heat of the sun," an allusion to the light and warmth of Torah. When a Jew studies Torah, he must do so with enthusiasm and excitement, recognizing that this is his connection to the essence of G-d.[3]

To See G-d

The second opinion[4] declares that the word Sivan translates as "to see." This alludes to the "Revelation," when the Jews were able to see G-d.[5]

Sin - Sinai

The Bal Haturim[6] explains that the reason we find the word Sinai written as "Sin" is because prior to receiving the Torah, the desert was referred to as Sin. When the Jews received the Ten Commandments, the letter Yud which equals ten, was added, thereby changing the word from Sin to Sinai. Sin was referred to as a desert, full of thornbushes. Upon acceptance of the Torah the Yud changed the desert into a holy environment and became Sinai.

As we mentioned in our discussion of Iyar, the letter Vav refers to Torah. In the Torah we find that the Yud and Vav are interchangeable.[7] The Rabbis added the letter Vav to the word Sin and formed the name Sivan, which indicates that during this month we became connected to Hashem at Mt. Sinai.

The Arizal[8] tells us that the summer and winter months are parallel. Nissan is connected to Tishrei; Iyar with Cheshvan; Sivan with Kislev, etc. Sivan is the month of Revelation. Chanukah begins on the 25th day of Kislev. The Rabbis explain that the holy candles of Chanukah reflect the light of Torah.

Torah Illuminates the Darkest Corners of the World

During the Hellenistic era, prior to the miracle of Chanukah, the Greeks tried, unsuccessfully, to convert the Jews to Greek philosophy. In Hebrew, the word for Greek is Yavan, which is spelled Yud, Vav, Nun. The name Sivan utilizes these same letters plus an additional Samech. The meaning of Yavan is mud, the combination of water and earth. Water symbolizes Torah. Earth reminds us of secular studies. It was the Greek's intention to combine Torah with their philosophy. The letter Samech, which means to "support," reminds us of Hashem's support of the Jewish people, and his reluctance to allow us to be "stuck" in the mud. Sivan gives us the strength to conquer the forces of negativity. The Hebrew letter that corresponds to Kislev, the month which is parallel to Sivan, is Samech. This reaffirms the power of Torah to illuminate even the darkest corners of the world.[9]

Humility - The Vessel for G-dliness

The numerical value of Sivan is 126. One hundred twenty-six is equivalent to the word Anov which is spelled Ayin, Nun,Vav. Anov means a "humble person." A Jew must recognize that everything he possesses is a gift from Hashem; his health, his wealth, and his well-being. In order to appreciate this gift, we must be humble.

The notion of humility is a prerequisite for studying Torah. The Midrash states that Hashem chose Mt. Sinai as the site of the Revelation, because of all the mountains in the desert, it was the smallest, a sign of humility. It was through Hashem's choice of the desert, for the giving of the Torah, that he taught the Jewish people to be humble. In the desert, one tends to feel lost and insignificant.[10]

The Blueprint of Creation

The Torah is not a historical book. The Torah reflects the brilliance of Almighty G-d and the blueprint of creation.[11] Hashem dressed Himself within Torah in order to enable us to connect with Him. Every time that we study Torah we unite with the essence of Hashem.[12] It is obvious, therefore, why in the beginning of this sacred book, Hashem revealed the purpose of creation as well as the holy mission of every Jew.

Our sages teach us that the purpose of creation was for the Jewish people to accept the Torah. This is emphasized with the first word of the Torah, which begins with the letter Bais, the first letter of the word Berashis which means "the beginning." Berashis is the combination of two words, Bais and Raishis,[13] "two Raishis." Raishis means "beginning." Hashem is marking the beginning of two entities: the Jewish people and the Torah. They set the standard for the world. As the prophet Isaiah said, the Jewish people must be a light unto the world. A Jew is, by definition, connected with Torah. The Torah is every Jew's vitality. It provides our essential life-force.

On the sixth day of creation, G-d concluded his work. The verse states: "Yom Hashishee." Grammatically, it should read, "Yom Shishee," without the extra Hay. This extra letter reveals a significant message. Hashishee means "the sixth day," an allusion to the famous sixth day of Sivan when the Jews received the Torah. This emphasizes that the culmination of the six days of creation was the Revelation of the Torah. Without the Torah, creation would lack purpose. We must accept that the giving of the Torah is a continuous process. Each time we are called up to the Torah we make a blessing and conclude by saying: "Boruch Atah Adonai Nosain HaTorah," which means "Blessed shall be G-d who gives us the Torah." We don't pray in the past tense, Nasan HaTorah, meaning "he gave us the Torah." Each day Hashem gives us His profound gift, which is the substance of Almighty G-d Himself, dressed in the words and lessons of Torah.[14]

Emes - Eternity

The word Torah begins with a Tof, which is the final letter in the Aleph Bais. Why should Torah, which declares the beginning of creation and sets the standard for the physical world, begin with the last letter of our holy language? The answer lies in the status of the Torah, which is referred to as Toras Emes, which means "the Torah is the absolute truth." The definition of truth is not only the opposite of falsehood, it also means something that will endure for all of eternity. The position of Tof, the last of the 22 letters, is reminiscent of the end of time. All material objects diminish, only the holiness of Torah lasts forever. In fact, not only is the impact of Torah and Mitzvahs infinite, their energies increase constantly.

The Tribe of Zevulun

The tribe corresponding to Sivan is Zevulun.[15] Zevulun means a "permanent residence." This refers to the holy temple and, symbolically, to the holy abode that is established by all Jews involved in worldly affairs. We all must emulate the tribe of Zevulun who brought G-dliness into the streets.[16]

The Final Nun, the last letter of the name Zevulun, reflects this concept. Nun equals 50, a reference to the giving of the Torah on the fiftieth day of the counting of the Omer. When transcribed, this letter extends below the line. This symbolizes the necessity for bringing the holiness of Torah to even the lowliest elements of society.

The Importance of Supporting Torah Study

Yaakov said[17] that the tribe of Zevulun will dwell on the coast and be involved in maritime affairs. Moshe said they will conduct their business with joy, and supply financial support to the tribe of Yisachar in their study of Torah. In fact the Torah discusses the blessing of Zevulun before Yisachar because it imbues honor on those who subsidize the study of Torah.[18]

The Emblem of the Ship

The flag of Zevulun was white and bore the emblem of a ship.[19] White symbolizes the happiness and joy the tribe experienced through their support of the study of Torah. Zevulun brought Hashem's message to the world. All business transactions were conducted in a Torah fashion, all matters of practical life were illuminated with the holiness of Hashem. This tribe fulfilled G-d's desire "to have a dwelling place in the physical world." Rashi tells us that the tribe of Zevulun had a profound impact on gentile merchants. They witnessed the sanctity and blessing of Hashem upon this tribe and were so moved that many of them converted.[20]

The symbol of the ship has a dual interpretation. On one hand, our holy sources tell us that the oceans refer to Torah. Just as water is essential to the survival of a human life, a Jew cannot spiritually exist without Torah. The image of the ship reminds us of our mission as Jews; we must learn to navigate in the holy waters of Torah and to explore all levels of learning.

On the other hand, some sources define the ocean as an intimidating and potentially dangerous place. A ship provides protection when traveling on unpredictable and powerful seas. Without this protection, we would find ourselves lost. Without the spiritual guidance of Torah and the performance of Mitzvahs, the Jewish people would be lost.[21]

The Mission of the Soul

The Ba'al Shem Tov explains the verse[22] "Yorday Hayom B'aniyois Oisay Melacha B'Mayim Rabim," meaning "those who go down in the sea with boats, and do work in the multitudes of water." This refers to the descent of the Neshoma into the physical body. Just as the sea conceals all that lays within the waters, the flesh envelops the soul. Every Jew must break through the limitations imposed by the body in order to experience his connection with Hashem.

Among those who descend into the sea, are some people who are fortunate enough to have vessels which provide security and protection. Unfortunately, others are vulnerable to the water's dangers. Similarly, some Jews are privileged and grow up in an environment defined by authentic Judaism. Others, however, lack the opportunity to benefit from a traditional education. Therefore, it is incumbent upon those who possess the boats and the life preservers to descend into the dark and murky waters. The knowledgeable Jews must reach out and rescue the lost souls.[23]

The Power of the Letter Zayin

The Arizal says that the letter Zayin is connected with the month of Sivan.[24] The word Zayin can be interpreted in three ways. The first meaning is "ornaments." The Talmud[25] tells us that at the time of Revelation each Jew received two crowns as a gift from Hashem. One crown was given because they said: "Nasa," meaning "we shall do the Mitzvahs." The second was given because they said "Nishma" meaning "we shall study and learn the reasons that we do the Mitzvahs." The Jews proclaimed Nasa before Nishma which teaches us that you must "do" even before questioning "why." This is the reason why Hashem rewarded us with crowns.

A crown is placed on top of the head. A Jew must transcend the limitations of rational thinking and intellect. He must accept Torah even before he understands. A crown is an ornament reserved for royalty. When a Jew accepts the study of Torah and the performance of Mitzvahs upon himself, he is connected with Hashem's crown, the essence of G-d. Each Jew becomes an entity of holiness and can offer guidance to the world in a kingly manner.[26] In Hebrew the word "crown" is Kesser. Kesser is equivalent to the numerical value 620, which is the exact number of letters in the Ten Commandments. In addition, the sum of the 613 Mitzvahs of the Torah plus the 7 which were added by our Sages of blessed memory, equals 620.

The second translation of Zayin is "sustenance." Torah is the true sustenance of each Jew. As Rabbi Akiva says, the connection of a Jew with Torah is like a fish with water.[27] Just as a fish cannot survive without water, it is impossible for a Jew to function properly without participating in the study of Torah. Another perspective on the sustaining powers of Torah involves our belief that the entire world receives its nourishment through the holiness of this study and the performance of Mitzvahs. As Maimonides states,[28] a Jew has to perceive the world as existing on a scale. Every time a Mitzvah is performed you have participated in balancing the scales towards the positive and allowing the world to grow in its strength and holy energy. Conversely, the same follows if you transgress.

The final translation of Zayin refers to "armor." This meaning is reflected in the mission of the tribe of Zevulun. In addition to their study of

Torah, this tribe also was involved in the world of commerce. The Rabbis refer to the interaction with worldly affairs as a "battle." The word Lechem meaning "bread" is related to the word Lochaim meaning "battle." In order to sustain oneself there is a constant struggle between physical and spiritual forces. A conflict arises when one tries to maintain one's sense of holiness and commitment to Torah law while at the same time struggling to succeed in business. This challenge is much greater in the business world than it is in Shul. The Jew's protective armor, which is worn to beat this adversary, is an intense involvement with the study of Torah and performance of Mitzvahs. The Torah is called Oiz which means "power" given to the Jew.[29]

The True Meaning of Walking

The human characteristic associated with this month is walking.[30] What is the significance of walking? Walking is an indication that there is life. As it is written[31]: "The Jewish people shall walk from strength to strength." A Jew must fulfill the full potential that Hashem granted him and always seek to advance his accomplishments. The connection with Torah is clear. Just as Torah is the life force of each Jew, "walking" is a metaphor for our constant growth through the study of Hashem's laws.

To Construct an Abode for Hashem

The verse in the Torah that corresponds to Sivan comes from the *Book of Exodus*:[32] "Yadosov U'litzela Hamishkan Hashaynis." We find Hashem's name when the first letters of these words are rearranged. This verse speaks of the building of the tabernacle during the time spent in the desert. This emphasizes the message of the month of Sivan; to bring the holiness of Hashem to the furthest reaches of civilization, and to construct an abode for G-d in these desolate regions.

TAMUZ

The Five Calamities Occurring on the Seventeenth of Tamuz • Seventeen Equals Good? • Tamuz Reveals the Deeper Dimensions of Hashem • G-d's Shield • The Garden of G-d • The Tribe of Reuvain: Love for Hashem •The Color Red • The Power of the Letter Ches • Fear of G-d • A True Understanding of Sight • Remaining Steadfast in Our Beliefs • Mordechai Did Not Bow

Moshe pleaded with Hashem, explaining that Exile had forced the Jews to live amongst the Egyptians and to be influenced by the practice of idol worship.

-- Midrash, Shmos Rabbah, ch. 43, v. 8

TAMUZ

The Five Calamities Occurring on the Seventeenth of Tamuz

The name of the fourth month of the Jewish calendar is Tamuz.[1] It is written in the Mishnah of the tractate Taanis,[2] that five calamities took place on the seventeenth day of this month at various times throughout history. The first, and most significant, occurred when Moshe came down from Mt. Sinai. After spending forty days and forty nights studying Torah with Hashem, Moshe received the tablets containing the Ten Commandments as a gift from G-d Al-mighty. Upon his descent from Sinai, Moshe saw his people worshiping the Golden Calf. In anger, he smashed the tablets. The consequences of this act are felt to this day. Our holy sources note that every generation of Jews must pay for this profound transgression.[3]

The second calamity that befell the Jews on this date was, that the daily sacrifice ceased to be offered, because the Jews no longer had sheep due to the war with the Romans. In addition, on this momentous date in Jewish history, the walls of Jerusalem were breached by the Romans, Apostmos burnt the Torah, and lastly, an idol was brought into the Temple .

Seventeen Equals Good?

The events occurring on the seventeenth of Tamuz, define this period as one of profound sadness. However, the Torah assures us that these days will be transformed into days of great jubilation upon the coming of Moshiach.[4] The Hebrew word associated with the number seventeen is Tov, meaning "good." (Tes = 9, Vav = 6, and Bais = 2). Why would a date on which such horrific events occurred be referred to as "good"? The answer is that ultimately this period is positive. We must have faith that its true nature will be revealed. These days contain tremendous energy which emanates from the infinite light of Hashem. Since the world is not prepared to receive such illumination at this time, the energy remains concealed until the arrival of Moshiach. This concept will be explored later during the discussion of the month of Av.

In the *Book of Ezekiel*,[5] we find a reference to an idol named Tamuz, who was, at one time, worshiped by the Jews. This clay idol was baked in the heat of the summer sun. It is noted that Tamuz was destroyed as a result of Hashem's wrath at the Jewish people for praying to a graven image. Why would the Rabbis choose the name of an idol as the fourth month of our calendar? This question can be answered by exploring a second interpretation of the name Tamuz.

Tamuz Reveals the Deeper Dimensions of Hashem

The literal translation of Tamuz is "heat." This alludes to the intense heat of the sun during this season of the year. In *Psalms*,[6] it is written that the heat of the sun is used as a metaphor for G-d's power. Hashem's strength expresses itself in two ways: creating positive energy and by destroying negative forces. Therefore, by using the name Tamuz, the Rabbis emphasize the infinite power of Hashem. Just as the idol Tamuz was destroyed by the wrath of Hashem, all negativity encountered by G-d will be mocked, and ultimately, destroyed. Hashem is always in control. The name Tamuz emphasizes a deeper dimension of G-dliness.[7]

G-d's Shield - The Garden of G-d

The numerical value of the name Tamuz is 453 (Tof = 400, Mem = 40, Vav = 6, and Zayin = 7). This number forms the word Tagain meaning "a protection or shield." This refers to Hashem's protection of the Jewish people from the dangers posed by our adversaries. Even during our darkest moments, when we find ourselves witnessing unbearable calamities, Hashem protects and nurtures us. When the letters of Tagain are rearranged, the word Ginas meaning "a garden," is formed. We find in the book *Song of Songs*,[8] the image of the garden is a metaphor for the love and pleasure that Hashem derives from the Jewish people. Just as the gardener who finds himself pricked by the sharp thorns on a rosebush, yet still stands in loving admiration of the plant's beauty, similarly, Hashem forgives His people for all transgressions, no matter how horrific. His love for us is unwavering.[9]

The Tribe of Reuvain: Love for Hashem

The tribe corresponding to this period of the Jewish calendar is Reuvain. The Torah[10] tells us that Reuvain sinned by moving his father's

(Yaakov) bed into his mother's (Leah) tent upon Rachel's death. Reuvain felt that his mother deserved the honor of being the primary wife of his father. Yaakov rebuked his son. He wanted to know who gave Reuvain the right to do such an act without his permission. Even though his intentions were good, Reuvain was ridiculed by his father. As a punishment, he lost the privileges of being the firstborn which Yaakov gave to Reuvain's brother, Yosef. Yosef, therefore, became the recipient of a double portion of land in Israel.[11] Rashi[12] quotes from the Midrash and tells us that Reuvain regretted this action throughout his life and repented vigorously via prayer and fasting. In addition, the Torah[13] tells us, that when Yosef was abducted by his brothers and about to be murdered, Reuvain saved Yosef's life. This noble act of courage elevated Reuvain. Instead of taking advantage of Yosef's vulnerability and becoming jealous that Yosef was the recipient of the birthright privileges, Reuvain saved Yosef and demonstrated his acceptance of Yaakov's decision.

The personality of Reuvain is reflected in the actions of his tribe. When the Jewish people were about to enter Israel after wandering in the desert for forty years, the tribe of Reuvain, together with the tribe of Gad and half of the tribe of Menashe, refused to settle in Israel. Their desire was to inhabit the west side of the Jordan River.[14] Moshe Rabainu ridiculed them for this choice. The tribes replied by clarifying their motives to Moshe. Their intention was neither to disrespect the holiness of the land nor to discourage others from entering Israel. They believed that since the ultimate victory of the Jewish people was dependent upon Hashem's intervention through miracles, their presence was not mandatory. Moshe replied that their contribution to the effort was essential. Hashem wanted the Jewish people to enter Israel as a united nation, and to be physically prepared to wage war. After Moshe reprimanded them, these tribes declared that they would be in the forefront of the army in the Jews' quest to conquer the land. Only after the Jews were victorious in their quest to claim the holy land as their own, would these two and one-half tribes return to their families on the other side of the Jordan River. Even though they made a poor choice which resulted in their being reprimanded, the final outcome revealed their actions to be noble.

The notion of being rebuked for an action and learning from the error, is similar to the events which occurred when Moshe broke the tablets on the seventeenth of Tamuz. Why? By destroying the tablets, the Jewish people learned to be humble and repented for their sin.[15]

In Chassidus, it is explained that the tribe of Reuvain is associated with love for Hashem.[16] When a Jew studies Torah and performs Mitzvahs, it is not sufficient to do so on a superficial level. One must do so with fervor. It is written in the first paragraph of the Shema: "You should love Hashem with all you heart, with all your soul, and with all your might."[17] This concept is reflected in the name Reuvain. When Reuvain was born, Leah said, "Re'U Bain," which means "look and you'll see my son."[18] In Kaballah, the concept of sight, or revelation, is associated with love of Hashem. To see Hashem is to connect with Hashem. The lesson of the tribe of Reuvain contributes a deeper dimension to our study of Torah and performance of Mitzvahs; all activities should be performed with love as a sign of our belief in Hashem's continuous presence in our lives.

The idea of love for Hashem is reflected in the month of Tamuz. When a person transgresses and then realizes his error, he reveals a deeper emotion because of his regret. Just as we find that the Jews who participated in the sin of the Golden Calf felt remorse, this act reinforced their commitment to serve Hashem and their intense love of Him.

This passionate commitment brings to mind the second segment of the word Reuvain, Ben, meaning a "son." Just as a child displays an unconditional love for his parent, the Jewish people serve Hashem with unlimited adoration.[19]

The Color Red

The color of the flag of the tribe of Reuvain was red.[20] The Rabbis tell us that the color red symbolizes Reuvain's shame for moving the bed of Leah.[21] Another explanation for this choice of color is that red is frequently associated with the heat and power of fire. This reminds us of the love Hashem demonstrated during Reuvain's act of repentance. The emblem found on the banner is the herb, Dudaim, which Reuvain found in the field and brought to his mother, Leah, for its fertility inducing powers.[22] Reuvain, a loving and caring child, felt his mother's grief because she no longer bore children and he wished to alleviate her pain. This concept of unconditional devotion reinforces the theme of the month of Tamuz; the love and passion that a Jew has for Hashem is a love of similar intensity to that which a child feels for his parent.

The Power of the Letter Ches

The letter associated with the month of Tamuz is Ches.[23] As we find in the prophet Ovadia, the letter Ches is used in the context of *breaking*. "Vichatu Giborecho," translates as "you break the strong one."[24] Breaking refers to the destruction of some of the symbols of the Jewish people: the tablets were smashed, the walls were breached, and the rituals were broken. The act of breaking also refers to Hashem's destruction of the idol, Tamuz, symbolizing the destruction of the negative forces found in the world.

The Fear of G-d

On the other hand, it says in the holy Kaballistic book, *Sefer Hatmuna*, the reference for the letter Ches comes from the word Chitas, which we find when the Torah describes the fear of G-d found in our enemies. Our adversaries avoided confrontations with the Jewish people because the fear of Hashem's wrath was paralyzing. This interpretation of the letter Ches also reflects the theme of the month of Tamuz. Hashem loves and protects His people, even in the darkest and most catastrophic of times. As noted previously, a seemingly disastrous act can be interpreted as a positive occurrence when examining the incident from a deeper perspective.

Another translation of Ches is to "ignite a fire."[25] Once again, this can be interpreted in two ways. Fire can be a sign of destruction and negativity. It also reminds us of the heat and passion that all Jews feel for Hashem.

A True Understanding of Sight

The characteristic associated with Tamuz, is that of sight. As with most of the concepts associated with this month, sight possesses dual interpretations. Sight can refer to control over our vision, for example, "don't give a bad eye,"[26] or "don't lust for another man's wife,"[27] etc. It is also through the eyes, however, that love is revealed. The significance of sight reminds us to open up our eyes to the realization what life is truly about: an awareness of all that Hashem gives us.[28]

Remaining Steadfast In Our Beliefs - Mordechai Did Not Bow

The verse that corresponds to the month of Tamuz is found in Megilas Ester: "Vichol Zeh Enenu Shaveh Lee."[29] The last letters of the final four words of this verse, when rearranged, spell out G-d's name. This verse speaks of Haman's arrogance towards Mordechai as he tells his family of the honor and glory he receives from the king. Even though Haman is proud of the recognition from the king, the kingly gestures are diminished since Mordechai does not bow to him. Eventually Haman and his sons were destroyed through the strength of Mordechai's leadership. We find once again the duality associated with the month of Tamuz. Haman's plot was to destroy the Jewish people. Ironically, he fell victim to his own scheme. As Jews, we have the potential to be steadfast in our beliefs. Just as Mordechai did not bow, we will transform sadness into jubilation.[30]

MENACHEM AV

The Five Calamities Occurring on the Fifteenth of Av • The Transformation of Sadness into Joy • Hashem Consoles Us, We Comfort G-d • The Numerical Value of Menachem • The Tribe of Shimon • Awe of G-d • The Color Green • The Mystical Meaning of the Letter Tes • The Message of "Hearing"

The Third Bais Hamikdash, Holy Temple, is constructed and will descend from heaven.

-- Rashi and Tosafos, Talmud Tractate Sukkah, p. 41A

MENACHEM AV

The Five Calamities Occurring on the Ninth of Av

The name of the fifth month of the Jewish calendar is Menachem Av.[1] The Mishnah[2] states that each year, as the month of Av begins, our sense of joy diminishes. The basis for this can be found in a discussion of the tragic events surrounding the Ninth of Av, known as Tisha B'Av.

The first tragedy which occurred on the Ninth of Av, is the story of the Jews who were punished by G-d and forced to die in the desert. Some of the participants in the Exodus from Egypt refused to enter the holy land, thereby inciting Hashem's anger. Our Rabbis offer several explanations as to why the Jews would choose to remain outside of Israel's borders. Some of the people feared the giants who inhabited the land at that time.[3] Others did not want to forfeit the comforts of the desert; the mana from heaven, being surrounded by the clouds of glory, etc. Still others did not want to enter because they would have to sacrifice the spiritual lifestyle they had followed, unchallenged by the demands of secular life. Their days were filled with the study of Torah and the performance of Mitzvahs.[4] It was on the Ninth of Av that Hashem decreed that all men, ages 20 through 60, must die in the desert. Since they had refused to enter Israel, G-d proclaimed that they would never live to see the holy land.[5]

It was on the Ninth of Av, at several points in our history, that we were admonished for not appreciating the gifts that G-d had bestowed upon us. Approximately 800 years after the Jews died in the desert, on the same date, the First Temple was destroyed. On exactly the same day, almost 500 years after that, we suffered the destruction of the Second Temple.[6] Approximately 60 years after the devastating loss of the Second Temple, Bar Kochva and his army were defeated and the city of Betar, the headquarters of the Jews, was demolished. Finally, years later, as it says in Jeremiah: "Zion was plowed like a field," on the Ninth of Av, and the city of Jerusalem was decimated.[7]

The Transformation of Sadness into Joy

Conversely, the fifteenth day of the month of Av, is one of the most joyous days of the year. It is written in the Mishnah in the Tractate

Tanis, that on the fifteenth of Av, in the fortieth year of the Exodus from Egypt, Jewish men ceased dying in the desert. On this date many years later, the Romans permitted the Jews who died at Betar to be buried. The Romans had refused burial privileges to those Jews. Our holy sources detail many other joyous events occurring on this date. It is customary that on the fifteenth of Av, because of the joyousness associated with this day, Jewish boys and girls meet potential mates.[8]

The Torah[9] tells us that on the first day of the month of Av, Aaron, the holy priest and brother of Moshe, passed away. Our Rabbis[10] tell us that we should learn from Aaron's example and love our fellow Jew, pursue peace, and bring Jews closer to the Torah.

Hashem Consoles Us, We Comfort G-d

The translation of Menachem Av is "being consoled by our Father, Hashem." A father loves his children unconditionally and hopes they will form a united front and help one another prosper. A father teaches his children of life's responsibilities through discipline. The love that is displayed through parental restraint is profound. The parent who is forced to scold a son or daughter often experiences more pain than the child.

Similarly, Hashem is our Father. Unfortunately, we did not appreciate the spiritual ecstasy of the Temples. It is written in the Talmud[11] that the Second Temple was destroyed and we still find ourselves in exile as a result of baseless hatred within the Jewish community. In order to receive the final redemption, we must rectify our sins by displaying unconditional love for our fellow Jews, as stressed by Aaron in his teachings. Hashem teaches us that while we wander in the Diaspora, it is through our commitment to the Torah that we will earn the right to return to the holy land.

The name of this month reminds us of the tragic events which occurred during this period. Even though we experienced profound suffering at this time, we must rely on our Father in heaven.

A second interpretation of the name Menachem Av is "to console our Father, Hashem." Our Rabbis[12] tell us that when Jews suffer, Hashem experiences the pain along with us. How do we console Him? We must comfort our Father, by studying Torah, performing Mitzvahs, and displaying unconditional love for our fellow Jew. These actions enable us to relieve His pain.[13]

The Numerical Value of Menachem

The numerical value of the word Menachem is 138, which equals the word Tzemach, one of the names of our righteous Moshiach.[14] The promise that Moshiach eventually will reveal himself is the ultimate way in which Hashem consoles us. The word Av, which means "father," is linked with strength. Our strength is that our father, Hashem, is always with us.

The connection between father and strength can be found in the numerical value of the word Av, equaling "three." In Jewish law,[15] the number three is associated with the word Chazoko, which indicates strength, permanence and stability. If a Jewish custom is performed three times, it becomes established and it is obligatory to follow the practice. Hashem promises us that we will achieve a sense of permanence through the strength of our connection with G-d, our Father.

Our sages point out that Tisha B'Av falls on the same day of the week as the first day of Pesach.[16] When Moshiach reveals Himself, this somber day will be transformed into a jubilant holiday. Just as Pesach is a time of redemption, we will experience emancipation on Tish B'Av. Our sages tell us that Moshiach was born on the Ninth of Av.[17] On the Ninth of Av, the Temple was destroyed. The Jews were then exiled and separated, metaphorically, from their partner in marriage, Hashem. On the other hand, the fifteenth of Av is a day of celebration which follows a period of intense mourning. The fifteenth of Av, traditionally a time for weddings, reveals the profound sense of hope which guides the life of every Jew; the promise of the ultimate wedding, our union with Hashem.[18]

The theme of the month of Tammuz, the period immediately preceding Av, emphasizes love for Almighty G-d. However, love of G-d alone is not sufficient. We also must stand in awe of G-d in order to fully connect with Him. This concept is reflected in the tribe of Shimon.[19]

The Tribe of Shimon • Awe of G-d

The tribe associated with the month of Av is Shimon.[20] The Torah[21] tells us that Leah, Shimon's mother, prayed for a child and upon giving birth, she said: G-d listened to my prayers. The root of the word Shimon is "Shoma," meaning *to listen.* In Chassidus, it is explained that there is a profound difference between *seeing and listening.* Seeing is associated with love for Hashem. Seeing makes one feels close to the experience, for example two friends meeting after a long separation. Listening is associated with an awe and fear of G-d.[22] When one merely listens, all actions are witnessed "second-hand" and lack the impact of seeing something "first-hand." In the spiritual realm, *seeing* evokes one's realization of how close G-d is to him, throughout all of his endeavors. This brings forth a tremendous love and passion for Hashem. However, *hearing* refers to one's recognition of how far he is removed from G-d, as a result of his transgressions. This creates a tremendous awe and fear of G-d Almighty. The fundamental prayer of the Jewish people begins with Shema Yisroel, "*Hear O Israel.*" The first level of spirituality that a Jew must attain is an awareness and an awe of G-d.

Shimon is perceived as a warrior. The Torah[22] notes that Shimon took revenge upon the city of Sh'chem, the home of the persons who assaulted his sister, Dina. Shimon sought to instill the fear of G-d in all nations so that these people could never again consider committing such atrocities. Although Yaakov, his father, reprimanded him for for what he considered to be improper behavior, the Torah recognizes Shimon for his courage.[24]

The Torah describes the terrible sins committed by the tribe of Shimon and the tribe's leader, Zimree. These men participated in acts of adultery with Midyinite women. As a result of these acts, tens of thousands of Jews died. This occurred during the fortieth year spent in the desert. Because of this transgression, Moshe, prior to his death, chose not to refer directly to Shimon when blessing the tribes of Israel.[25]

The association of this tribe with the month of Av is obvious. Jews suffered a tremendous loss through the transgressions of the tribe of Shimon, just as it was during the month of Av that Jews suffered many calamities. Shimon personifies the fear of G-d, and an understanding of the month of Av enhances our awe of Hashem.

The Significance of "Green"

The color of the flag associated with this tribe is green.[26] Green recalls illness, a sign of the sickness the tribe of Shimon suffered upon being punished for their monumental sins. The emblem on the banner was the city of Sh'chem. This serves as a reminder of the zealous acts of Shimon, the founder of the tribe, who fought against adultery.

The Mystical Meaning of the Letter Tes

The letter associated with Av is Tes.[27] According to the Midrash,[28] Tes alludes to Tit, meaning "mud" and is symbolic of the earth, from which man's body was created and to which it will ultimately return. This connection reinforces the concept of awe of G-d. When we humbly accept that, ultimately, we will return to the source of our conception, our awe of G-d and acknowledgement of His power is intensified.

In the sacred book of Kabballah, called Sefer Hatmuna, it is written that the letter Tes alludes to a verse in Isaiah: "Viteetayseeha Bimatatay Hashmayd," meaning "G-d will sweep with his broom and eradicate." On one hand, the letter Tes reminds us of G-d's infinite power to destroy anything which stands in opposition to His will. The destruction of the Temple came during the month of Av and was a result of the Jewish people's failure to fulfill G-d's will. On the other hand, the verse also speaks directly to any enemies of the Jews, who sought to eradicate us. They would be punished by Hashem. This coincides with the theme of Menachem Av, G-d's consolation to the Jewish people.

The Talmud[29] tells us that if a man sees the letter Tes in a dream, it is a sign that good will befall him. The first appearance of this letter in the Torah is in the word Tov, meaning "good."[30] The association of the letter Tes with the month of Av supports a concept previously discussed; even though many calamities befell our people during this period, Hashem assures us that he will not forsake us and that, ultimately, all will be good.

It is significant to note that Ches is the letter associated with Tammuz, the month preceding Av. When we combine Ches and Tet, we have the word Chet, meaning "sin." It was because of our transgressions that we were forced to experience all of the calamities identified with these two months.

The numerical value of the letter Tes is nine. This number alludes to the Ninth of Av. The number nine often is associated with the nine months of pregnancy. Pregnancy is, metaphorically, similar to Golus, meaning "exile." Just as a child is concealed in the mother's womb, there is a concealment of G-dliness throughout the Diaspora.[31]

The Message of "Hearing"

The characteristic of the month of Av is *hearing*.[32] We employ this sense when listening to the words of Hashem. We also should listen to one another in order to avoid conflicts within our own community. We should not, however, listen to gossip. This sin led to the destruction of the Second Temple, which occurred during the month of Av.

There are two verses associated with Av. The first is: "Hinai Yad Hashem Hoya Bimiknecha," meaning "the hand of G-d is present in your cattle."[33] This verse alludes to one of the plagues visited upon the Egyptians prior to the Exodus. Hashem destroyed their livestock. This indicates Hashem's wrath, but at the same time, reveals His kindness. Even though he killed the cattle, at that time, he did not kill the Egyptians. He afforded them the opportunity to repent and correct their ways. Similarly, during the month of Av, Hashem dispensed His anger upon the Jewish people, while at the same time, He revealed his kindness. It is written in the Midrash,[34] that G-d released his wrath upon the stones and wood of the Temple, not G-d forbid, upon the Jewish people.

The second verse associated with this month is: "Haskeis Ushma Yisroel Hayoim," meaning "pay attention and listen, Jew, to G-d today." The connection with the month of Av is clear. The tribe of the month, Shimon, is connected with the act of *listening*.

ELUL

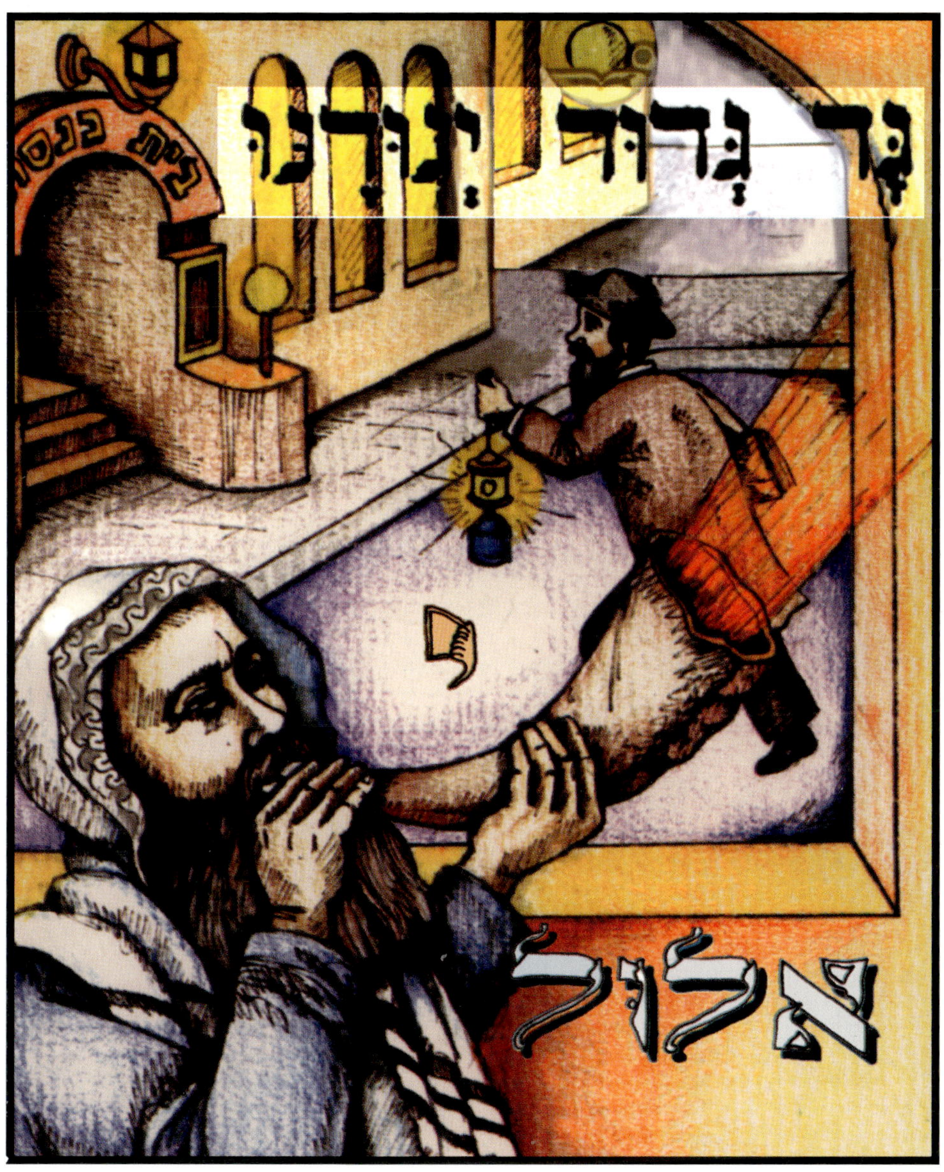

Moshe Ascends for the Second Tablets • The Twenty-fifth Day of Elul: The Day of Creation • Torah: The Purpose of Creation • The Five Acronyms of Elul • Torah • Tefillah • Acts of Kindness • Repentance • Moshiach • The King In The Field • The Tribe of Gad • Mana • Black and White: The Colors of the Flag of Gad • The Power of the Letter Yud • The Virtue of Victory • The King Reveals His Essence • Charity or an Obligation?

The Mitzvah of Tzedakah is of such a profound nature, that it initiates the Final Redemption.

-- Talmud Tractate Baba Basra, p. 10A; Shabbos, p. 139A

Moshe Ascends for the Second Tablets

On the first day of Elul,[1] the sixth month of our calendar, Moshe ascended Mt. Sinai to receive the second set of tablets containing G-d's commandments.[2] The forty days and nights that followed the Revelation of the Torah had culminated with Moshe descending from Sinai with the first tablets containing G-d's laws As we know,[3] he smashed these holy relics after witnessing his people worshipping the Golden Calf. Shortly after he broke the tablets, Moshe prayed to Hashem on behalf of the Jewish people. He then ascended to heaven a second time, for another forty days, and pleaded for G-d's compassion, imploring Hashem not to destroy the Jews and to bless them with a second chance to repent. On the first day of Elul, Moshe ascended for a third time, in order to receive the second set of tablets. He descended from the mountain on Yom Kippur with the second set of tablets containing the Ten Commandments. Just as the first Yom Kippur revealed Hashem's mercy as he forgave the Jews for their sins by awarding them a second chance to repent, this holiest of days, which falls on the tenth day of Tishrei, is the culmination of Moshe's forty days of learning and serves as a Day of Atonement for future generations.[4]

The Day of Creation

It was on the twenty-fifth day of Elul that G-d created the world.[5] Rosh Hashanah, the first day of the month of Tishrei, was the sixth day of creation. It was on this day that G-d created Adam. Six days prior to this miraculous event, the twenty-fifth of Elul, is when the process of creation began. The mission of creation is to imbue the physical world with the study of Torah and the performance of Mitzvahs.[6] This is emphasized during this forty day period, beginning on the first of Elul and ending on Yom Kippur, the tenth day of Tishrei.

Torah - The Purpose of Creation

The Torah[7] speaks about the sixth day of creation: "Yom Hashishi Vayichulu Hashamayim V'Haaretz," meaning "On the sixth day, G-d completed the heaven and the earth." The Rabbis teach us that the first four letters of these words spell out Hashem's name. Hashem's presence was revealed, in the physical world, through the completion of His work which culminated on Shabbos.

The Talmud[8] states that, grammatically, it is not necessary to include the letter Hay in the word Hashishi. The Talmud declares that the letter Hay emphasizes the importance of this day in our history. This word Hashishi, not only indicates the sixth day of creation, it also reminds us of the sixth day of the month of Sivan, when Hashem revealed the Ten Commandments. G-d created the world, on the twenty-fifth day of Elul, on the condition that it would be imbued with Torah. The Jews received and accepted the Torah on Yom Kippur. Throughout the month of Elul, the Jews repented and declared their willingness to accept the Torah.

The Five Acronyms of Elul

The name of this month has numerous interpretations. As our learned Rabbis[9] tell us, the word Elul appears as an acronym at least five times in the Torah, representing five themes.

Torah - The theme of Torah appears in the first acronym: "Ina Liyodo Visamtee Loch."[10] which means "it happened to you (inadvertently) and therefore you shall establish (places of refuge)." The Talmud[11] explains that the study of Torah provides security and refuge for every Jew.

Tefillah - The importance of prayer is revealed in the second acronym: "Ani Lidodi Vidodi Lee,"[12] meaning "I am to my beloved and my beloved is to me." It is during prayer, that we connect with our Father in Heaven and our love and passion for Hashem intensifies. This inspires G-d's love. Our sages explain that the final letters of these four words all end with the letter Yud. Yud equals ten. Four times ten equals forty, a reference to the forty days which began on Rosh Chodesh Elul and ended on Yom Kippur.

Acts of Kindness - The third acronym relates to acts of kindness: "Ish L' Reahu U'matonos L'Evyonim,"[13] meaning "A person to his friend and gifts to the poor." This significant verse stresses our responsibility to help one another in order to elicit G-d's help.

Repentance - The fourth acronym teaches repentance: "Umal Hashem Es L' Vavcha V'Es L' Vav Zarecha," meaning "You shall circumcise the foreskin of your hearts and your offsprings hearts."[14] This is the concept of Teshuva, when we become sensitive to our purpose in life and the responsibilities that we have to our creator.

Moshiach - The final acronym for Elul is connected with the final redemption through Moshiach. It comes from the song sung by the Jews after the splitting of the sea during our Exodus from Egypt. The initial letters of the words "Vayomru Laymor Ashira L' HaShem,"[15] meaning "We will sing to Hashem in the following way," when rearranged, form the name of the month of Elul. The sages[16] tell us that the process of our final redemption began with the Exodus from Egypt. The Talmud[17] teaches that there is a reference to the concept of "T'Chiyas Hamaysim," the resurrection of the dead, a principal doctrine of Judaism, in this portion of the Torah. The song begins: "Az Yoshir Moshe Uvinay Yisroel," meaning "Moshe and the Jewish people sang to Hashem." In the Hebrew grammar, the proper word used when describing the act of singing in the past tense is Shor. The use of the word Yoshir, which contains an additional Yud, changes the word from past to future tense. The significance of this combination of tenses reveals that Moshe and those who followed him out of Egypt, will be resurrected and sing to Hashem with the coming of Moshiach.

The numerical value of Elul is 67. The word Binah, meaning understanding, also has a numerical value of 67.[18] Binah contains two words, Ben, meaning son, and Yud-Hay, meaning G-d. Since every Jew is a child of Hashem, we each are blessed with an understanding and insight into our mission in life. Our essence is revealed within the aforementioned Torah verses for which Elul is an acronym.

The King In The Field

In the month of Elul, Hashem reveals himself to every Jew. Even though this month has no official holidays we are told that throughout the month there is a holy force of energy that shines upon us. The parable for this reality is about a king who resides in palace throughout the year. However once a year he goes out amongst his people to greet everyone in a friendly manner. Everyone has the opportunity to welcome the king without permission of servants and guards. Similarly Hashem, the King, comes out to be with his people and shows a smiling face to every Jew.

The Tribe of Gad

The tribe associated with the month of Elul is the tribe of Gad.[19] Before passing away, Yaakov blessed all of the tribes of Israel. He gifted Gad with the power and strength to overcome their enemies.[20] As we know,[21] this tribe settled on the other side of the Jordan River, across from the land of Israel. They entered the holy land and lead their brothers in their quest to conquer the land. We also find[22] that Moshe blessed the tribe of Gad with the capacity to be great warriors. Moshe admired them for the *Tzidkas*, righteousness, which they exhibited when they stood in the forefront and lead the Jewish army in its mission to conquer the land.
Moshe had a vision that he would be buried in the portion of land controlled by the tribe of Gad. He was buried in this tract of land because he embodied the essence of Gad - love for his fellow Jews, even if it involved great personal risk. In the Torah[23] we find that when the Jews sinned with the Golden Calf, Moshe beseeched G-d to forgive the Jews for their great transgression. Moshe said to Hashem: "If you don't forgive the Jews, erase my name from the Torah." Therefore, it was appropriate for Moshe to be buried in the land controlled by the tribe of Gad as they frequently demonstrated tremendous sacrifice for their fellow Jews.

The Talmud[24] tells us that the letters Gimel and Dalet, which form the name Gad, are an acronym of two words: Gomel Dalim, meaning "to help the poor." This reinforces the concept of offering assistance in a time of need. We also find Gad used in reference to the mana. The Torah[25] says: "V'Hamon Kizra Gad Hu," meaning "the mana was round like the physical seed called Gad." The mana illustrates Hashem's blessings which enable us to pursue a livelihood and support our families. A Jew must know that, ultimately, the success of his Parnasa, making a living, depends on Hashem's kindness. In order to receive Hashem's kindness, we must share our blessings with others.[26] This concept is embodied in the actions of the tribe of Gad.

Black and White - The Colors of the Flag of Gad

The flag of the tribe of Gad is a combination of black and white threads.[27] Black and white symbolize that although this tribe was constantly exposed to war, indicated by the black, they were triumphant in their endeavors, indicated by the color white. The emblem found on the banner is that of military troops. In accordance with Yaakov's prophecy, this tribe would lead the Jews in the battles fought to conquer the holy land.

The Power of the Letter Yud

The Hebrew letter corresponding to this month is Yud. The letter Yud is the smallest letter found in the Hebrew alphabet. This indicates humility. A Jew must be humble and sensitive. G-d's name begins with the letter Yud. As our Rabbis tell us,[28] Hashem reveals Himself to those who are humble. Every Jew has an innate connection to Hashem. We find this connection demonstrated through the use of the letter Yud. This letter is found at both the beginning of Hashem's name and the names commonly used to refer to the Jewish people (Yisroel, Yehudim, Yaakov, etc.), a royal position not given any other letter in the Hebrew alphabet. The physical smallness of this letter, when compared with the other letters in the alphabet, does not diminish its holiness. The same can be said about the Jewish identity.

The pronunciation of the letter Yud is reminiscent of the word Yad, meaning "hand."[29] Once again, we are reminded of our obligation to extend our hands, metaphorically, to our brothers. In order to feel another person's pain we must be sensitive. This profound attribute finds its roots in a Jew's humility.

In the sacred book, *Sefer Hatmuna*, it is written that the Yud alludes to a specific verse in Tehillim:[30] "Yoidu L'Shem Chasdoi," meaning "Give thanks to Hashem for His kindness." This coincides with all of the aforementioned concepts. When a person is humble, as is the letter Yud, he recognizes his limitations and gives gratitude and thanks to Hashem for His kindness. Recognizing Hashem's benevelence motivates us to reach out and share Hashem's blessings with our fellow Jews.

The Virtue of Victory

The personal trait linked to the month of Elul is Nitzochon, meaning "victory."[31] Every Jew faces a constant battle, his essence versus the secular world, in his quest to maintain his holiness.[32] The Yetzer Hara, the evil inclination, is always ready to ambush the Yetzer Tov, the good inclination. It is our duty to be alert and aware of our holy mission and conquer our adversary. We achieve this formidable task with the assistance of G-d Almighty. Our sages[33] tell us that if Hashem did not assist us in this fight for holiness we would not succeed in conquering the mighty power of the Yetzer Hara. We merit Hashem's assistance and strength by being kind to others; the spirit of the month of Elul.

The King Reveals His Essence

Once again, we are reminded of the connection between the different elements of the month. Just as each individual Jew must participate in a battle to ensure the holiness of his soul, the tribe of Gad fought to ensure that the Jewish people maintained their domination of the holy land. There is a famous parable which demonstrates the objective of the Jewish nation. There was once a King who inherited priceless treasures from his ancestors These treasures were hidden from the public and high level officials. However, when it came to war, these treasurers were sacrificed in order to achieve the ultimate goal of victory. The lesson is that the King is Hashem. The battle is between holy forces and the negative influences. The soldiers are the Jewish people, as the Torah[34] tells us, every Jew is a soldier in Hashem's army. It is our mission to succeed, even if it means that the King has to sacrifice His treasures.[35] Hashem reveals his essence to us to conquer the Yetzar Hara.

Charity or an Obligation?

The Torah verse corresponding to the month of Elul is "U'Tzedakah T'Heye Lanu Kee," meaning[36] "Hashem will do Tzedakah (Righteousness) with us when we keep Hashem's Mitzvahs." The translation of the word Tzedakah usually defined as charity, is inaccurate. The literal translation is righteousness.[37] Charity means performing beyond the call of duty. The Torah tells us, however, that Tzedakah is an obligation and the responsibility of every Jew. Therefore, when fulfilling this important Mitzvah, a Jew is serving his fellow Jews as he is required. Nevertheless, Hashem rewards us for our acts of Tzedakah, as if they were voluntary and not an obligation.[38]

TISHREI

Yerech H'Aysanim: The Strong Month • The Significance of the Number Seven • Tishrei: To Release • The Letter Tav and Teshuva • Rosh Hashanah: The Creation of Adam • The Cry of the Shofar • Yom Kippur and the Ten Commandments • Sukkos Reveals Our Appreciation of Hashem's Blessings • Lulav and Esrog • Jewish Unity • Simchas Torah and Our Love for Hashem • The Tribe of Efraim • Joshua: A King and a Teacher • Efraim: A Jew in the Diaspora • The Color Black and the Image of the Bullock • The Mystical Meaning of the Letter Lamed • Intimacy: A Sacred Act • Neutralizing the Negativity

The Mitzvah of Teshuva, returning to G-d, is so powerful that it inspires the arrival of Moshiach.

-- Talmud Tractate Yoma, p. 86B

TISHREI

Yerech H'Aysanim - The Strong Month

The seventh month of the Hebrew calendar is Tishrei[1]. We find in the *Book of Kings*,[2] this month is called Yerech H'Aysanim, "the strong month." This is an allusion to our patriarch Avraham, who is vital to the spiritual forces of this month. The Torah refers to this month as Hachodesh Hashve'e, meaning "the seventh month."[3] Our Rabbis tell us that the word Shve'e has a second interpretation which comes from the word Soiva, meaning "saturated."[4] According to the Midrash,[5] the number seven is very significant. As we know, Shabbos falls on the seventh day of the week, the sabbatical year is the seventh in the cycle, and Tishrei, the seventh month of the calendar, is saturated with holidays.

Tishrei - To Release

In Aramaic, Tishrei means "to release."[6] Hashem frees us from our debts accrued during the year and excuses our transgressions. By doing Teshuva, returning to a life of holiness, Hashem releases us from punishment for our sins. A second interpretation alludes to a spiritual release. Even though a Jew may study Torah and perform Mitzvahs throughout the year, he is still limited in his ascension, since learning is based upon intellect. During the month of Tishrei, however, we are able to achieve the highest level of spirituality and transcend these boundaries.We are then able to touch the essence of the Divine. The spirit of G-d transcends all degrees of holiness attainable throughout the rest of the year.[7] During Tishrei, the soul releases itself from all constraints and achieves its destination. It is during this month that Hashem reveals Himself to every Jew.[8]

The Letter Tav and Teshuva

The first three letters of Tishrei are the final three letters of the Hebrew alphabet, written backwards. If a Jew has fallen to the lowest level of spirituality, reflected by Tav, the most distant letter from Aleph, the first letter of the alphabet, he is encouraged to return to his roots. During the month of Tishrei, a Jew does Teshuva, studies Torah and prays, Tefillah, all beginning with the letter Tav, and works his way back home to Hashem, represented by the letter Yud, the final letter in Tishrei.

The Creation of Adam

The first holiday of this month is Rosh Hashanah, translated as "The Head of the Year." Just as the brain controls the nerves which coordinate the entire body, Rosh Hashanah impacts the entire year.[9] It was on the first day of Tishrei that Hashem created Adam. The Midrash[10] states that on the same day Adam was created, this first man gathered together all forms of life, including wildlife and vegetation, and proclaimed Almighty G-d as the King of the Universe. Every year on Rosh Hashanah, we too, crown Hashem as our King.[11]

The Cry of the Shofar

The blowing of the Shofar on Rosh Hashanah also awakens our Jewish soul and unites us with Hashem. The Shofar releases a cry that awakens compassion and mercy. It is the wordless appeal of the Neshomah, the soul, yearning for its source, pleading for forgiveness and to be united with Hashem. Words are limited and cannot convey the depth of our emotions. By communicating with G-d through the holy Shofar, we are able to evoke the consent of the King to accept our prayers and continue his sovereignty.[12]

Yom Kippur and the Ten Commandments

On the first Yom Kippur, the Jews commemorated the giving of the Torah and the descent of Moshe from heaven with the second set of tablets. Just as G-d forgave the Jews who transgressed by worshipping the Golden Calf, which led to the destruction of the first tablets, this day was established as a day of forgiveness for future generations.[13] Hashem gave the Jews a second chance because they demonstrated true Teshuva. The essence of G-d, the essence of the Jewish people, and the essence of Torah are one entity.[14] On Yom Kippur the spirit of the Jew touches Almighty G-d through the process of doing Teshuva.[15]

The essence of Torah is reflected in the tablets containing the Ten Commandments. Hashem's laws were not written upon the stone. They were engraved within the stone. When one writes on paper, the script and the paper are two separate entities and can be divided by erasing the words. However, when a stone is engraved, the letters become one with the stone, and cannot be divided unless you destroy it. The Ten Commandments were engraved on stone to reinforce the concept that G-d and Torah are one entity.[16]

The Ten Commandments embody the essence of G-d. Torah is G-d's brilliance, Yom Kippur was the appropriate day for Hashem to reveal his love for the Jewish people by sharing His essence with us, through His gift of Torah. Since Yom Kippur was the day that the Jews did Teshuva and touched the spirit of Almighty G-d Himself.

Sukkos Reveals Our Appreciation of Hashem's Blessings

On Sukkos, the fifteenth day of Tishrei, Hashem commands us to sit in a temporary dwelling.[17] We must vacate the comfort of our homes for a cycle of seven days. In order to appreciate our good fortunes throughout the year, we relocate for this period and live in temporary discomfort, thereby acknowledging Hashem's blessings. Another lesson derived from the Festival of Sukkos is that a Jew must realize that everything he possess in the physical world is temporary. Only the study of Torah and the performance of Mitzvahs are of everlasting value.

On Sukkos we are commanded[18] to perform the Mitzvah of Lulav and Esrog. The Lulav is a branch of the palm tree. The Esrog is a citron. We tie together the leaves of a myrtle, a willow, and a palm tree. We then make a blessing. The Midrash[19] says that these four species represent the four types of Jews. The Esrog represents a Jew who studies Torah and does Mitzvahs, the Lulav represents the Jew who studies Torah but does not perform good deeds, the myrtle symbolizes the Jew who performs good deeds but does not study Torah, and finally, the willow reflects the Jew who neither studies Torah nor performs Mitzvahs. This act unites these species and creates one entity. Similarly, Hashem yearns for all Jews to be connected.

The eighth day of Sukkos is called Shemini Atzercs.[20] The Midrash says[21] that this day is designated for Hashem to celebrate, exclusively, with the Jewish people. In Israel, this day also is celebrated as Simchas

Torah. During the Diaspora, the celebration extends through the following day. We express our love for Hashem and our joy of being Jewish by dancing with the Torah. The Torah contains a level of holiness which is unparalleled.

Simchas Torah and Our Love for Hashem

On Simchas Torah, every Jew is invited to participate in the joyous celebration. Every man receives an Aliyah, regardless of his level of observance. This reemphasizes the connection that every Jew has with the Torah. As it is explained in *The Code of Jewish Law*, even a person who does not understand Hebrew is called up to the Torah for an Aliyah and makes a blessing.[22] Even though he does not intellectually understand the meaning of the words, his Neshoma transcends these limitations and connects with the words being read.

Three fundamental elements of Judaism are underscored throughout the month of Tishrei: to accept Hashem as our King, to return to G-d through Teshuva, and the significance of Torah. These three principles also are reflected in the tribe of Efraim, the tribe associated with the month of Tishrei.[23]

The Tribe of Efraim

The Torah[24] tells us that the reason that Yosef named his son Efraim was: "Kee Hifrani Elokim B'Eretz Onyee," meaning "Hashem made me multiply in the land of my suffering." Although Yosaif endured difficult times in Egypt, he conquered the sorrow and pain of being kidnapped and imprisoned for 13 years, through his faith in Hashem. The concept of neutralizing negativity is similar to Teshuva. By undertaking the process of Teshuva, we depart from a state of spiritual bankruptcy and return to our roots. During Rosh Hashanah and Yom Kippur, we acknowledge what we lack spirituality and welcome the opportunity to "return home."

Spiritually, a Jew is liberated from his Yetzer Hara, evil impulse, during the High Holiday period. The Talmud[25] tell us that Yosaif was released from prison on Rosh Hashanah. The Torah relates the story that Yosaif brought his children, Menashe and Efraim, to his father, Yaakov, for the final blessing before Yaakov passed away. Yaakov placed his right hand on Efraim and his left hand on Menashe even though Menashe was older. Yosaif had placed Menashe on Yaakov's right side in order for him to receive the blessing with the right hand of his grandfather. Yaakov, however, criss-crossed his hands and blessed Efraim first. Yaakov had a vision which foretold that Joshua, who would descend from Efraim, would be the one to lead the Jews into Israel and teach them Torah. Therefore, Efraim had priority over his older brother.[26]

Rashi[27] tells us that Joshua was a king. Joshua conquered other kings and governments to enable the Jews to settle in the land of Israel. Joshua, a king and a teacher of Torah, reflects the spirit of the month of Tishrei, the time when we accept Hashem's sovereignty and reinforce our commitment to Torah.

In Likutei Torah,[28] the Alter Rebbe explains that just as the Jews were instructed to make a covenant with Hashem promising to accept the precepts of Torah before entering the land of Israel, every year before we enter the new year on Rosh Hashanah, we each must reinforce our covenant with Hashem. Once again, we see the connection between Joshua, the Jewish leader who led the Jews into the holy land, with the month of Tishrei.

Efraim - A Jew in the Diaspora

In T'NACH,[29] we also find a reference to the Jewish people being called Efraim. During our prayers in the Musaf of Rosh Hashanah we quote the famous verse: "Habain Yakir Lee Efraim," meaning Hashem speaks with an intense love to the Jewish people and he says "How dear are you, Jewish people to me." This refers to the love that the Jews demonstrated throughout the Exodus. They had complete faith in Hashem and entered the wilderness with no shelter, no protection, and no security. Just like Efraim, who grew up with his brother Menashe in Egypt, a decrepit society completely void of moral values, Efraim still maintained his Jewish identity. He therefore symbolizes the Jew who lives in the Diaspora, an environment which lacks Torah values and spirituality. Nevertheless, the Jewish spirit remains firm and strong with faith in Hashem.

The flag of the tribe of Efraim was black and portrayed a picture of a bullock.[30] The color black was a sign of Yosaif's pain and misery. The bullock was a symbol of the strength of Yosaif's tribe to conquer the land through the leadership of Joshua.

The Mystical Meaning of the Letter Lamed

The letter Lamed, which is connected with the month of Tishrei,[31] means both "to teach" and "to learn." This reinforces the connection with the month of Tishrei. During this month, a Jew must commit himself to a higher level of Torah study, including the obligation to share his knowledge with someone who is less informed. He declares an appreciation of Hashem through the gift of being educated in Torah.

A second translation of the letter Lamed comes from the words Malmad Habakar, meaning "the teacher of the cattle."[32] The cattle goad that spurs the animal into movement is called Malmad. This teaches us that it is insufficient just to study Torah if it remains abstract.[33] The laws of Hashem must permeate the physicality of our daily existence and civilize our animalistic nature in order to elevate us to a higher purpose. The letter Lamed is the tallest letter in the Hebrew alphabet, a symbol of Hashem's majesty. Hashem is the King of all Kings. He is above and beyond all of creation.

The numerical value of the letter Lamed is 30. As it is explained in *Pirkei Avos*,[34] a king has 30 levels, advantages, over a commoner. The final word contained in the Torah is Yisroel, which ends with the letter Lamed. This teaches us that when a Jew, Yisroel, studies Torah, he is elevated to the highest levels.[35]

Intimacy - A Sacred Act

The personal trait associated with Tishrei is intimacy,[36] alluded to in the translation of the name Efraim, which means "to multiply." The Talmud[37] tells us that there are three partners in the creation of a child: the father, the mother, and Hashem. In Judaism, intimacy is not perceived as a promiscuous act. It is a sacred part of fulfilling our mission in life.[38] During the month of Tishrei, when a Jew is imbued with holiness, he infuses even the lowest act with G-dliness. Intimacy is no longer an animalistic act, it has evolved into a holy mission. This concept is reflected in the Bris, covenant, that Hashem makes with every

Jew. The Bris, circumcision, is located on the organ that procreates to teach us that we must elevate the lowest levels to the highest plateaus. The Talmud[39] tells us that women are born with an advantage over men, they do not need the circumcision for the covenant, it is innately instilled within them. We must recognize that by imbuing holiness into the mundane, we acknowledge Hashem's absolute control.

Neutralizing the Negativity

The verse corresponding to the month of Tishrei is "Va'yiru Oisa Soray Paroh"[40] meaning; "And Pharaoh's officers saw Sara." Avraham and Sara went down to the land of Egypt because of the famine in the land of Israel. When Pharaoh's officers saw the beauty of Sara, they abducted her and brought her as a gift to their king. Miraculously, Sara was returned to Avraham untouched and they proudly returned to the holy land. It is explained in mystical sources that on Rosh Hashana, the Day of Judgement, the negative forces in the spiritual realm act as prosecutors in the heavenly courts. These forces are associated with Pharaoh and his people. Avraham and Sara advocate on our behalf in order to neutralize these evil spirits. Just as Sara was sent home with honor and dignity, we are promised a peaceful and blessed new year.[41]

MARCHESHVAN

Mar - Bitter! • Mar - The Rainy Season in Israel • The Third Bais Hamikdash Will Be Dedicated During MarCheshvan • Mar-Cheshvan Is Called Bul • The Seventh of Cheshvan - Jewish Unity • The Challenges of This Month • Rain Is Dependent Upon Our Behavior • The Tribe of Menashe • Menashe and Neshama • The Color Black and Its Message • The Power of the Letter Nun • The Transformation of Golus • Rayach - To Serve Hashem With Joy • To Rejuvenate Our Consciousness • The Third Temple

Hashem withholds the gift of rain, because of those who publicly commit to give Tzedakah, and fail to do so.

-- Talmud Tractate Taanis, p. 8B

MARCHESHVAN

Mar - Bitter! The Rainy Season In Israel

In the Mishnah,[1] the eighth month of the Jewish calendar is referred to as MarCheshvan. One of the translations of Mar is bitter.[2] This month is lacking the sweetness derived from holidays. A second translation of the word Mar comes from "Mar Midlee," meaning "drops of water." This is the rainy season in Israel.[3] Mar also means "sir" or "master." It is explained in the Midrash that King Solomon finished building the First Temple during the month of MarCheshvan. The building was not inaugurated for eleven months until the month of Tishrei, the following year. Hashem rewarded the month of MarCheshvan by promising that the third Bais Hamikdash, which will be revealed with the coming of Moshiach, will descend from heaven and be dedicated during MarCheshvan.[4] Therefore, we refer to this period with the respectful titles of "master" and "sir" as we must honor the period which marks our greatest joy.[5] Linguists say that the word Cheshvan traces its roots to "Chashras Mayim," meaning an abundance of water.

It is my belief[6] that the root of this word also alludes to the word Chash, meaning "something that comes with speed." As we know,[7] in Israel it is on the seventh day of this month that, in our daily prayers, we begin asking Hashem for rain. Unfortunately, throughout history the land of Israel has suffered many droughts. As the Mishnah[8] relates, there were numerous occasions when the Jews observed fast days in order to plead for rain. In fact, most of the Tractate Taanis is devoted to these days of fasting and praying for rain. In the Shema,[9] Almighty G-d promised the Jewish people as a reward for doing Mitzvahs, he will provide rain at the proper time. G-d forbid, the punishment for transgressions will be suffered through droughts. Rain is a crucial element for our survival. Therefore, the name of this month, is appropriate. We need an abundance of rain and we hope and pray for its speedy appearance.

The Holy Rabbi Yisroel from Ruzin explains that the name of this month can be read with different vowels. In Aramaic, MarCheshvan means "the movement of the lips."[10] During the month of Tishrei, the time when a

Jew is consumed with praying and beseeching Hashem, and consumed in the intense study of Torah, his mouth becomes a conduit for G-dliness. The impact of these holy vibrations of the lips are still felt in the month of MarCheshvan.

MarCheshvan Is Called Bul

In *The Book of Kings*,[11] this month is called Bul. The word Bul has several meanings: 1) This is the root of the word Mabul, the flood of Noach, which began during this period; 2) Bul is also the root of the word Novoil, meaning to be tired out. This alludes to the seasonal change indicated by withering and falling leaves; 3) Bul also means "large holes." As the rains assault the earth, they often cause trenches and puddles.

The letter Mem was added to the word Bul, forming the word Mabul, because it equals forty, a reference to the forty days during which the flood encompassed the earth. Our sages[12] tell us that although, at first glance, the flood came to destroy the world, upon deeper analysis we realize that the flood came to purify it. Jewish Law[13] requires that a Mikvah, must contain a measurement of forty S'Ah, approximately 200 gallons of water. The number forty also reminds us of the forty days that Moses was in heaven receiving the Torah.[14] The world needed to be cleansed spiritually, as if the entire earth was immersed within a holy Mikvah, in order to reach a higher level and receive G-d's gift of the Torah.

Jewish Unity

On the seventh day of this month the Jews begin to pray for rain. Our Rabbis tell us that all Jewish men were obligated to make a pilgrimage to Jerusalem on Sukkos. They returned home immediately after Shemini Atzerets, the 22nd of Tishrei. The most distant community in the holy land was found along the Euphrates River and took fourteen days to reach from Jerusalem. In order for these men to travel safely and not be pelted by the heavy rains of the season, the Jews did not begin their prayers for rain until the seventh of MarCheshvan, thereby ensuring the safe return of *all* the Jewish men. The Jewish people are connected and form one entity. As long as one Jew lacks comfort, the entire Jewish community bends in order to accommodate him.

The Challenges of This Month

The month of MarCheshvan is the time when we fulfill our mission of "V'Yaakov Holach Lidarko," meaning "and Yaakov went on his way."[15] Yaakov is the name of every Jew. After the climax of the High Holy Days - Rosh Hashanah, Yom Kippur, Sukkos, Shemini Atzerets, and Simchas Torah - when we are inspired by our spiritual experiences, we are commanded to imbue the mundane and simple days of the year with this energy, in order to elevate them to a higher level. It is during this month that we must utilize the strength accumulated during Tishrei. The challenge is great. We are entering the winter, when the nights are long, dark, and cold, reminding us of a lack of spiritual warmth. We must learn from our forefather, Yaakov, who left his father's house, and traveled on his own, as it is detailed in the Torah.[16] He achieved spiritual growth through his individual efforts, without the benefit of living within the holy house of his parents.

Rain Is Dependent Upon Our Behavior

As is mentioned in the Shema, rain is a natural force that is dependent upon our behavior. If we behave in an appropriate manner, Hashem gives us the gift of rain. The difference between rain and dew is that dew never ceases to be produced.[17] For rain to be produced it must go through the process of the clouds collecting vapor and releasing it,[18] the process begins from below to above. This is similar to a Jew's spiritual development as he ascends to higher levels. Dew symbolizes Hashem's blessings irregardless of our behavior which is declared in his covenant with the world,[19] specifically the process of creation which never ends.[20] Therefore, during the month of Nissan, we thank G-d for dew. During the month of MarCheshvan we ask for rain.[21] Nissan is the time when the Jewish nation was newly born.[22] Like a baby who must be sustained by his parents, we require nourishment unconditionally, just as dew unconditionally nourishes the earth. As we attain higher levels of G-dliness throughout the month of Tishrei we enter MarCheshvan *deserving* the gift of rain.[23]

The Tribe of Menashe

The tribe corresponding to the month of MarCheshvan is Menashe. Menashe was the oldest son of Yosaif. As the Torah[24] tells us, "Key

Noshani Elokim Es Kol Amolee V'ais Kol Bais Avi" meaning "Hashem makes me jump away from forgetting my father's house." When Yosaif lived alone in Egypt, prior to the arrival of his father and brothers, he named his son Menashe. Yosaif wanted to constantly remember his identity. His son was named Menashe as a reminder not to be absorbed in his own problems and, G-d forbid, forget his roots.[25] This concept is apropos with the month of MarCheshvan. When a Jew exits the month of Tishrei, he finds himself in a spiritual vacuum after experiencing the intense holiday period. A Jew must always be aware of his roots and "jump away" from the negative influences which surround him.

When the letters used to spell the name Menashe are rearranged, we find the word Neshoma meaning "the soul."[26] When a Jew is in touch with his Neshoma he will not forget his Father in Heaven.

The Color Black and Its Message

The flag associated with the tribe of Menashe was black and displayed the image of a ram's horn.[27] The color black reminds us of the difficult times suffered by the tribe of Menashe. Over a period of time, there were five Kings appointed from this tribe, which resulted in tremendous internal strive amongst the Jewish community.[28] The ram's horn refers to Gideon, a descendant of Menashe, a leader of the Jews who was in the forefront of many battles.[29] This reminds us of the spiritual war we all wage during the month of MarCheshvan.

The Power of the Letter Nun

The letter associated with this month is Nun,[30] meaning "to perpetuate."[31] The root of the letter Nun is Nin, meaning a "descendant." An heir <u>perpetuates</u> the legacy of his forefathers. One of the names of Moshiach is Yenon, similar to Ye-Nun, since the coming of Moshiach will be the culmination of all the generations of Jews and will perpetuate the eternal nature of the Jewish people.[32] In Aramaic, the word <u>Nuna</u> Yama means "the fish of the sea." Once again, we are reminded of the time of the great flood. Our Rabbis tell us that the fish survived the flood which took place during this month.[33]

The Hebrew alphabet contains two letters called Nun; one which bends and is used at the beginning or middle of a word. The second, is straight and descends below the line, and comes only at the end of a word. The Talmud[34] tells us that these two Nuns refer to the "faithful one who is bent" and the "faithful one who is erect." One who serves the Almighty with humility, bending before Him (the bent Nun), will be rewarded on the final day of judgement as he stands upright (the final Nun).

A second interpretation of the bent Nun refers to our service of Hashem, who we approach with awe. Just as a servant approaches his master with fear, we kneel before Hashem and accept His sovereignty with the proper respect. The final Nun symbolizes our steadfast service before Hashem, performed with a heart full of faith that everything will turn out well.[35]

The Transformation of Golus

The Talmud[36] tells us that the letter Nun stands for the word "Nefillah," meaning to "fall." This refers only to the bent Nun. The final Nun represents redemption, the antithesis of falling.[37] In the portion of *The Book of Numbers* (Bamidbar),[38] that deals with the Jews traveling through the desert with the Aron Kodesh, the holy ark, Moshe declares "Kumah Hashem." This means "G-d is standing up," indicating that the Clouds of Glory were rising above the Jewish camp and beginning to move forward. An inverted Nun is found just prior to this Torah portion and immediately following it. The mission that the Jews assumed by traveling through the desert with the holy ark was to neutralize the negative forces represented by the desert,[39] an environment lacking water and vegetation. A spiritual void exists in this arid climate. The Jew must imbue even the lowest elements with G-dliness. The inverted Nun symbolizes the transformation from Nefillah, "falling," to Geula "redemption" thereby transforming darkness into light. As we see, the word Aron (Ark) ends with a final Nun. The final Nun extends below the line signifying the impact of G-dliness even in the lowest levels. MarCheshvan also ends with a final Nun, emphasizing the transformation of the spiritual disaster of the great flood into the positive aspects of purifying the world. As it is written in Isaiah:[40] "When Moshiach comes, the world will be filled with the knowledge of G-d as the sea is covered with water." This concept is also alluded to through the second meaning of the letter Nun, "fish," which is associated with water.

Rayach - To Serve Hashem With Joy

The characteristic of this month is Rayach,[41] meaning a fragrance or good smell. This teaches us that we must serve Hashem with pleasure and enjoyment just as a good scent gives us pleasure. We must ensure that we bring Hashem much Naches, from us, His children. As it says in the Torah, G-d receives much pleasure when he observes His children following His commandments and living according to His laws.[42]

To Rejuvenate Our Consciousness

Another benefit of a Rayach, or potent scent, is that by placing it directly under our nostrils, it awakens us from a deep sleep or, G-d forbid, loss of consciousness.[43] In the spiritual sense, during the month of MarCheshvan, when there is a lack of festivals and spiritual excitement, we must rejuvenate our consciousness by being more cognizant of Hashem and His Mitzvahs.

The verse in the Torah which corresponds to this month is "U'dvash Hayom Hazeh Hashem."[44] This verse speaks of the Jews entering the holy land and G-d's instructions to them to keep His Mitzvahs. The word U'dvash means "honey." Honey is pleasurable, and reminds us to serve Hashem with joy and vigor.

The Third Temple

We find in Tenach,[45] that the evil king of the Ten Tribes, Yerovom, declared a holiday for idol worshipping on the fifteenth of this month. This signified our falling to the lowest levels. However, we have the ultimate promise and guarantee of Hashem that by serving Him with joy, we will once again, enter the holy land and we will feel the holy presence of G-d in the Bais Hamikdash.

KISLEV

Chanukah - To Dedicate • The Battle With the Greeks • The Soul Is the Light of G-d's Candle • To Be A Light Unto the Nations • The Lights of Chanukah Neutralize All Negativity • Kislev Means Security • Chanukah Activates the Light of Creation • The Tribe of Benyamin • The "Holy of Holies" • The Flag of Benyamin And Its Multi-Colored Hues • The Secret of the Letter Samech • To Sleep With Holiness • The Funeral of Yaakov • Every Jew Is A Soldier • True Religious Freedom

Those who fulfill the Mitzvahs of the Chanukah and Shabbos candles, will be rewarded with the blessing, that their children will be imbued with Torah.

-- Code of Jewish Law Tur, #671;
Talmud, Shabbos, p. 23B

The ninth month of the Hebrew calendar is Kislev.[1] The miracle of Chanukah occurred during this period in Jewish history.

Chanukah - To Dedicate • The Battle With the Greeks

During the Hellenic Period, the Jews suffered socially, economically, and spiritually under the oppressive policies of the Greek Empire. The Greeks forbade Jews from circumcising their newborn sons, outlawed the observance of Shabbos, and made it impossible for Jewish couples to follow the laws of family purity. Many Jews lost touch with their identity and assumed Greek culture as their own. Ultimately, the Greek presence defiled the most holy of Jewish sites, our holy temple, the Bais Hamikdash. As our Rabbis tell us,[2] when the Greeks infiltrated the Holy Temple, all sacred vessels, including the oil used to burn the Menorah, became contaminated. Finally, a small group of holy priests, Kohanim, led a revolt against the Greeks. They called themselves Maccabees, an acronym for Mee Chamocha B'Aileem Hashem, meaning "Who is as strong as you, G-d?" Their faith in Hashem inspired the tremendous courage needed to revolt against the mighty Greek Empire. After many battles, the Jews reclaimed and rededicated the Holy Temple. The translation of Chanukah is "to dedicate."[3]

When the Jews entered the Holy Temple, the only jug of oil bearing the seal of the High Priest, the Kohen Gadol, was found hidden under the ground. The oil in the container was only enough to sustain the light in the Menorah for one day. Miraculously, the flames burned for eight days and nights.

Our Rabbis[4] pose the question: "Why is this holiday celebrated by lighting candles? Why don't we commemorate the victories of the Maccabees with food and drink?" The Greeks were not interested in destroying our physical beings or eliminating our presence in Israel. They sought to claim the Jewish soul. They welcomed Jews in the holy land as long as they lived according to Greek culture. The definitive battle was not instigated by the Greeks, it was the reaction of Jews who could no longer endure the spiritual holocaust. The holy priests fought to ensure the preservation of the Jewish soul. We celebrate the victory of the Maccabees through lighting candles. Light is a spiritual element within the realm of physicality. Light is not subject to the limitations imposed by gravity; it constantly creates energy which is a manifistation of Hashem's power.

The Soul Is the Light of G-d's Candle

Lighting the Chanukah candles is a spiritual act possessing tremendous energy. It is written:[5] "Ki Ner Mitzvah V'Torah Ohr" meaning "A Mitzvah is like a candle and the Torah is the light." By lighting the candles of the Chanukah Menorah we celebrate the immortality of the Jewish soul. It is said[6] that "the candle of Hashem is the soul of man." Through the study of Torah and the performance of Mitzvahs, we ignite the spark of holiness that exists within each Jew. At the same time, we illuminate the darkness of the secular world. In our pursuit of higher spiritual levels, we must not forget our responsibility to the rest of the world. We serve as a light unto all nations.[7] The laws detailing the lighting of Chanukah candles differ from those corresponding to the lighting of Shabbos candles. The candles which are lit to welcome every Shabbos, must be burning within our homes near our Shabbos tables, *before sundown*. The number of candles remains constant. On Chanukah, however, we light the Menorah which is placed by the window or doorway *after sundown*. The number of candles increases with each additional day of the holiday.

The reason for these differences is profound. On Shabbos the world is infused with G-d's holiness. Even after the sun sets and the physical world is enveloped in darkness, it is still illuminated by spiritual light. We do not have to brighten the streets. Shabbos does that for us. We don't have to increase the number of candles as the Sabbath provides that element.

The Lights of Chanukah Neutralize All Negativity

The festival of Chanukah occurs during the week, therefore the majority of the days do not benefit from the intense light of Shabbos. The world remains dark. We must assume the Mitzvah of lighting our candles after sundown in order to illuminate the darkness of the negative forces. These negative elements are not easily conquered. In order to ensure victory, we increase the light on each night and display the Menorah ablaze with positive energy upon our doorpost to neutralize any negativity.[8]

Kislev Means Security

Kislev means security and protection.[9] The Jewish people experienced Hashem's shelter through the miraculous events of Chanukah. Kislev consists of two words; Kas and Loi, meaning "a covering to Him (Hashem)."[10] Prior to the events surrounding Chanukah, G-dliness remained concealed. Kislev, the security and protective powers of Hashem, freed us from our adversaries.

To Be A Light Unto the Nations

The Miracle of the Oil reflects how we can reveal what was once hidden. Light reveals the Truth. We must squeeze the olive to reveal its essence, (the oil). By lighting the Chanukah candles we liberate G-dliness from its concealment and enlighten the world.

Chanukah Activates the Light of Creation

"Loi" equals 36. Thirty-six is the total number of candles we light on Chanukah. A deeper examination reveals a connection between the 36 Chanukah candles and the 36 hours encompassing the first Shabbos of creation. Our Rabbis tell us that the sun did not set on the first Shabbos. The light remained throughout the twelve daytime hours of Friday, the twelve nighttime hours of Friday, and the twelve daytime hours of Shabbos. Chanukah commemorates and activates the intensity of the light of the first Shabbos.[11]

Our Rabbis tell us that it was on the twenty-fifth day of Kislev, when the Jews concluded the construction of the Mishkan, the tabernacle in the desert, which commenced immediately after Yom Kippur. Hashem instructed Moshe to delay the dedication of the Mishkan until Rosh Chodesh Nissan (the first day of Nissan). The month of Kislev was compensated with the rededication of the holy sanctuary through the miracle of Chanukah.[12]

The Tribe of Benyamin

The tribe corresponding to the month of Kislev is Benyamin.[13] Benyamin was the only son of Yaakov born in the holy land. His name translates as "the son of the south." Rashi explains that Yaakov traveled south from Aram Naharaim, located in the north, on his journey to the holy land. A second translation of Benyamin is "son of my old age," alluding to Benyamin's birth during the latter years of his father's life.[14]

Our Rabbis tell us that the Bais Hamikdash was built on the portion of land belonging to two tribes, Yehuda and Benyamin. The "Holy of Holies," which contained the Ten Commandments, was constructed on Benyamin's land. How did Benyamin become so fortunate? The Midrash offers three explanations. Benyamin was the only child of Yaakov to be blessed by being born in the holy land of Israel. A second reason is that since he was not involved in the kidnapping of Yosef, Benyamin remained holy and pure and served as the proper receptacle for G-d's glory. Finally, the Midrash proposes a parable for the third explanation of Benyamin's good fortune: The father of many children will someday find his home empty as his progeny embark on their adult lives, with the exception of the youngest son, whose duty it is to stay home and assist his aging father. At the same time that his brothers were occupied with personal matters, Benyamin devoted himself to his father, Yaakov. The selflessness and virtue of Benyamin laid the foundation for the holy presence of the Bais Hamikdash on land belonging to his tribe.[15]

Yaakov shared his visions of what the future held for the tribe of Benyamin. He foresaw the victories of King Saul and the events surrounding our observance of Purim. Both King Saul and Mordechai, leaders who saved our people from the threats of our enemies, were descendants of Benyamin.[16]

The connection between the tribe of Benyamin and the month of Kislev is apparent. Hashem chose the parcel of land belonging to Benyamin as the location of the Bais Hamikdash, a site forever imbued with holiness. The miracle of Chanukah occurred in the Holy Temple. Yaakov's visions of King Saul and Mordechai underscore the theme which unites these leaders with the story of Chanukah: Hashem's commitment to His people, even in the bleakest of times. The lessons of the month of Kislev emphasize G-d's promise never to forsake the Jewish people. The cloak of Hashem protects us and enables us to remain strong in the face of oppression. The miracle of the oil reveals the profound level of holiness found within the Jewish soul. Our spirit, like oil combined with other elements, always rises to the top.

The Multi-Colored Flag of Benyamin

The flag of Benyamin combined the colors of all twelve tribes of Israel and the emblem was a wolf.[17] The multi-colored cloth united the Jewish nation to receive the blessings of Hashem. The Holy Temple was constructed on Benyamin's land which brought blessings to the entire Jewish nation. A wolf "snatches" its prey and the remaining carcass satisfies its hunger. The sacrificial altar found in the Holy Temple blessed the entire Jewish community through heavenly flames which seized and consumed the holy offerings of the physical world. The altar, which represents the Jewish people, served to conquer the world for Hashem and reveal the truth concealed in the physical world. The altar gives us the strength to "snatch" and elevate the holy sparks found within the realm of physicality before the negative forces contaminate them.[18] It is said that upon the arrival of Moshiach: "The wolf will dwell with the sheep."[19] Hashem will then abolish all negativity and holiness will envelop the world.

The Secret of the Letter Samech

The letter associated with this month is Samech.[20] Samech means "to support or encompass." The Midrash[21] tells us that Hashem constantly sustains the entire universe. If Hashem withdraws his energy, even for one second, all of creation would dissipate. The Midrash[22] associates the letter Samech with the Holy Temple and the Jewish people, who sustain themselves on their own merits and those of their ancestors.

The second meaning of Samech, to encompass, is reflected in its shape. A Samech is closed and circular. Like the never-ending lines of a circle, the Shechina, the divine presence, which revealed itself in the Bais Hamikdash, is everlasting. This gift from Hashem will endure throughout eternity and, thereby, ensures the never-ending existence of the Jewish people.

The word Nes, meaning "miracle," combines the letters Nun and Samech. Nun symbolizes falling,[23] Nefillah. Samech means to support. When these two letters are combined it emphasizes that miracles occur when collapse appears imminent. Hashem supported the Maccabees and, miraculously, they prevailed and rededicated the Holy Temple.

To Sleep With Holiness

The attribute of the month of Kislev is Shina,[24] meaning "to sleep." The Midrash[25] says every night when a Jew goes to sleep, his soul ascends to study Torah with Hashem. As a person sleeps, his animalistic inclinations lie dormant as the Yetzer Hara rests. The Neshoma, then emerges from its hiding place and connects with G-d.

Every Jew Is A Soldier

Every Jew is a soldier in Hashem's army.[26] A warrior serves his country at all times. His conduct must be impeccable as he represents his nation. A soldier sleeps only to regain his strength and continue his fight with renewed vigor. It is the duty of each Jew, after a night's rest, to serve Hashem with never-ending joy.[27]

Prior to the time of Chanukah, the Jewish people lacked spiritual consciousness. The miracle of Chanukah woke us from our slumber and allowed us to experience our inner essence and reconnect with Hashem.

True Religious Freedom

The Torah verse connected to Kislev is "V'Yar Yoshaiv H'Oretz H'Kinani," meaning "The inhabitants of the land of Canaan saw."[28] When our patriarch Yaakov passed away, his children brought his body from Egypt to Israel in order to bury him. The people who lived in the land of Canaan witnessed the funeral procession, which occurred on Chanukah, seventy days after Sukkos.[29] Rashi tells us that the many leaders of the land of Canaan were about to engage in battle when they encountered the sons of Yaakov at their father's funeral. Upon seeing the crown of Yosef, the Viceroy of Egypt, these warring rulers removed their crowns in respect. During the month of Kislev the Jews witnessed the defeat of their enemies and celebrated true religious freedom.

TEVES

The Translation of the Torah Into Greek Equated to the Sin of the Golden Calf • Ezra HaSofer's Leadership • The Siege Upon Jerusalem • The Fast of the Tenth of Teves • The Power of the Number Ten • The Symbolism of Iron • Teves - Good! • Teves and the Yahrtzeit of Abraham • Samson and the Tribe of Dan • The Color Sapphire • Nachash - Snake and Moshiach? • The Letter Ayin and Its Esoteric Meaning • The Eye of Yaakov Versus the Evil Eye • Anger Is Akin to Idolatry • Ity - To Praise Hashem Together

Why was the First Bais Hamikdash destroyed? Because of three transgressions: idolatry, adultery, and murder.

-- Talmud, Tractate Yoma, p. 9B

TEVES

The tenth month of the Jewish calendar is Teves.[1] During this period we commemorate three sorrowful events which occurred on consecutive dates during this month.

The Translation of the Torah Into Greek

On the eighth day of Teves, during the year 312 B. C. E., King Ptolemy ordered our elder Rabbis to translate the Torah into Greek.[2] This caused the Jews great sorrow.The Torah is our heritage. Except for the laws concerning non-Jews, gentiles are forbidden to study Torah.[3] As long as the Torah was written only in Hebrew, its sanctity was secure. Once it was translated into Greek, however, Hashem's holy messages were vulnerable to abuse by our enemies. Rabbis were forced to debate priests and bishops over the interpretation of verses in the Torah. Jews were persecuted because of inaccurate translations. Our sages compare the eighth of Teves to the day when the Jews constructed the Golden Calf. Just as the Golden Calf brought much pain and spiritual degradation upon the Jewish nation, the translation of the Torah into Greek was the beginning of a succession of calamities that befell the Jewish people.[4]

Ezra HaSofer's Leadership

On the ninth day of Teves in approximately 307 B. C. E., Ezra HaSofer, the great Jewish leader, passed away.[5] After the First Temple was destroyed by Nebuchadnezzar of Babylon in 422 B. C. E., the Jews lived in exile for seventy years. It was during this period that the Persian emperor rose to power and we witnessed the miraculous events celebrated during Purim. After our liberation from the tyranny of Haman, approximately 42,000 Jews returned to the holy land of Israel and the second Bais Hamikdash was built. Several years after the construction was complete, Ezra returned to Israel from Persia where he studied Torah with his teacher, Boruch Ben Neriah, who was the disciple of the prophet Jeremiah. Upon his arrival in the holy land, Ezra was shocked to witness the spiritual bankruptcy of the Jewish community. Many Jews were married to non-Jews and ignored the laws pertaining to the holy Shabbos. Ezra convinced the Jews to return to their heritage and to repent for their transgressions. He also was instrumental in organizing the construction of the walls surrounding Jerusalem.[6] Our sages[7] tell us that Ezra was worthy of receiving the Torah, had Moshe not preceded him. The death of Ezra was a source of tremendous grief.

The Siege Upon Jerusalem

On the tenth of Teves in 425 B. C. E., Nebuchadnezzar, the wicked one, layed siege upon Jerusalem. This onslaught led to the destruction of the Temple two and a half years later and set in motion the events leading to the exile.[8]

The Fast of the Tenth of Teves

Our Rabbis tell us that if the tenth of Teves occurs on a Shabbos, it is mandatory that we observe the fast. All other fast days, with the exception of Yom Kippur, are delayed until Sunday. Why does this day possess the power to void the Mitzvah of eating on Shabbos? The tenth of Teves is the *initial* event in the series of calamities befalling the Jewish people. All other calamities are a continuation of this bitter day. This day saw the initial breakdown of the Jewish community which lead to the future exiles and the destruction of the Bais Hamikdash. Therefore, it is essential that we abstain from all festivities and reflect upon the occasion.[9]

The Hebrew word for besiege is Somach, which also means "to support." Hashem sent the Jews a message through a gentile, beseeching them to support one another. By re-establishing their connection to each other they would experience spiritual growth. The Jews were united through the attack. This was Hashem's incentive for the Jews to repent and regain their strength. Hashem gave us the opportunity to amend our negative behavior in order to receive His blessings.[10] Brotherhood is the vessel through which we receive His sanctification.

The Power of the Number Ten

The day of the attack, the tenth day of the tenth month, is also connected with the final redemption.[11] The number ten possesses great power. Yom Kippur is observed on the tenth of Tishrei.[12] Hashem gave us the Ten Commandments. Ten Jews are required to form a Minyan. The Torah says[13] that the Jewish people sang to Hashem nine times, the tenth time will announce the coming of Moshiach. All of the aforementioned emphasizes the deeper meaning of the tenth of Teves. We now observe this day in a solemn manner. This day, however, embodies the power of the number ten which possesses the potential to transform darkness into light, and sadness into joy. Unfortunately, the Jews did not utilize the benefits of this catastrophic situation and return to Hashem. Consequently, the purpose for the destruction of the Temple was to bring our people, through the pain of exile, to a higher level through Teshuva.

The Symbolism of Iron

The prophet Ezekiel experienced a vision[14] which revealed the destruction of the Bais Hamikdash. Hashem instructed Ezekiel to place an iron frying pan between himself and the walls of Jerusalem, as a sign that the city and the Temple would be destroyed. The Torah[15] states that iron is a symbol of destruction. Since it is used to construct implements of war, it is not permitted to be used inside the Bais Hamikdash, a sanctuary of peace. An iron tool would nullify the holy altar. The sign of the iron, however, will be neutralized with the construction of the Third Temple when all negative elements will be transformed into positive ones. We will use iron to build the sanctuary and declare the strength of Almighty G-d who transforms swords into plows.[16] By renewing and strengthening the ties that connect the Jewish community through the process of Teshuva, we will merit the Third Bais Hamikdash, which will last forever.

Teves - Good?

The name Teves is similar to the word Tov, meaning "good." There are references in the Torah[17] to times when our Rabbis take great efforts to avoid all negative comments and use only positive language. Since Teves marks the beginning of the calamities of Jerusalem, the sages named this month Teves to inspire thoughts of goodness in order to activate Hashem's positive energy. We neutralize all negativity by referring to this month as Teves, "good." Another example of our using positive energy to nullify negativity is found[18] in the naming of the month of Av, which means "father," thereby implying compassion. The destruction of the Temple, an act which lacked humanity and compassion, occurred on the Ninth of Av. In order to infuse this month with the spirit of Hashem's mercy, it was named Av.

Teves is the combination of two words, Tes and Bas .[19] Tes means "nine," a reference to the Ninth of Av, the culmination of the tenth of Teves. Bas means "daughter." In Tanach[20] there are many references to the term "Bas" (Bas Yerushalayim, Bas Tzion, etc.). The Jewish people and the holy city of Jerusalem are referred to as Bas, meaning "the daughter of Almighty G-d," an allusion to what was experienced by the Jewish people and the city of Jerusalem on the Ninth of Av.

The Yahrtzeit of Abraham

Avraham Avinu passed away during this month.[21] The Torah[22] states "Tikovair B'saiva Toiva," meaning "he passed away at an old age." When rearranged, the first three letters of these words spells Teves. Avraham was the first Jew. His faith, which inspired many to believe in the sovereignty of Almighty G-d, illuminated the world.[23] Upon his death during the month of Teves, a darkness fell upon the world.

Samson And the Tribe of Dan

The tribe associated with the month of Teves is Dan.[24] Yaakov said[25] that Dan will judge the Jewish nation, a reference to Shimshon (Samson), a descendant of Dan. Shimshon was a judge for twenty years, while at the same time bravely fighting against the enemies of the Jews. Our enemies feared this formidable warrior for forty years; twenty years while he was alive plus an additional twenty after his passing. Yaakov prayed for Shimshon to lead the Jews to victory. Yaakov endowed Dan with the power of a serpent. Just as a serpent is able to attack its prey with its poisonous venom, Shimshon destroyed his foes with his dynamic strength. Dan, meaning "judgement," reminds us of Hashem's harsh judgement because of the actions of our people during this month.

As the Jews traveled through the desert, the tribe of Dan trailed the other tribes.[26] They would retrieve lost objects and return these items to their rightful owners. Since their position was at the end of the camp, Dan was often attacked by enemies of the Jewish people. Dan required a special blessing from Yaakov to overcome these dangers. Moshe referred to Dan[27] as a lion. He imbued them with the leadership qualities associated with the king of the beasts.

The Midrash[28] states that this tribe was consumed with the practice of idolatry. As stated in Genesis,[29] when Avraham Avinu battled with the four kings, he chased them until he reached the place called Choiva/Dan. Rashi tells us that Avraham had a prophecy revealing that the tribe of Dan would worship idols at this location. This realization weakened Avraham and he returned home. The Pesel Michah, the idol of Michah, was found in the city ruled by the tribe of Dan.[30] The wicked King Yeravam erected an idol in his image in the land of Dan.[31] The sum of all of this negative energy emanating from Dan sets the tone for the calamitous events occurring during the month of Teves. On the other hand, the positive energy associated with the victories of Shimshon infuses this month with the power to defeat the negativity.

The Color Sapphire

The color of the flag of Dan was sapphire,[32] an allusion to the darkness which defined the spiritual behavior of this tribe. The emblem was a serpent, referring to the power of Shimshon. The Torah[33] compares Dan to a Nachash, meaning serpent or snake. When rearranged the letters spelling Nachash form the word Choshen, the holy breastplate worn by the high priest, the Kohen Gadol.[34] We are reminded that is is possible to transform the lowest elements (a serpent), into one of the highest example of G-dliness (the high priest). The numerical value of Nachash is 358, the same as Moshiach. Once again, we see that this month possesses the potential to transform exile into redemption.

The Esoteric Meaning of the Letter Ayin

The letter corresponding to the month of Teves is Ayin.[35] The Talmud[36] tells us that Ayin is an abbreviation of Aniyim, meaning "poor people." Ayin follows Samech in the Hebrew alphabet and is significant since Samech means "to support." We must all fulfill the Mitzvah of supporting the poor. Assistance should be offered not only in the form of money, it also should be spiritual and emotional help. The month of Teves is poor because it marks the beginning of a series of Jewish calamities. During this period, when we mourn the destruction of the Holy Temple, we require special assistance from Almighty G-d.

Ayin translates as both "eye" and "fountain." Eyesight is an essential sense. The Talmud[37] tells us that a blind man is likened to a dead man. The eyes reflect a person's essence similarly, the Bais Hamikdash reflected the essence of Hashem. It was at this holy site that the divine presence was revealed. Eyes also are associated with light. The holy sanctuary enlightens the world.

The Evil Eye

Unfortunately, an eye also can be utilized for evil. Ayin Hara, the evil eye, occurred during this month. We are blessed with the holy eye of Yaakov which infuses fountains of blessings.[38]

The second translation of Ayin, "fountain," represents life. Water is referred to as Mayim Chaim,[39] "living water." Water which bursts forth from a natural spring is pure. The Bais Hamikdash is the life force of the entire world.[40]

Anger Is Akin To Idolatry

The characteristic of this month is anger.[41] Once again, we witness the harsh judgement and wrath of Hashem. Our Rabbis[42] warn us that anger is akin to idolatry. A Jew must maintain control over his emotions at all times.

To Praise Hashem Together

The verse corresponding to the month of Teves is "G'adloo L'Ashem Ity U'niromimo Sh'moi Yachdov",[43] meaning "Exalt Hashem with me and let us praise His name together." The numerical value of the word Ity, meaning "with me," is 411, the same numerical value as the word Teves. By praying together and being unified as a nation we will receive the blessings of Hashem, and ultimately, the final redemption.[44]

SHEVAT

Moshe Teaches the *Book of Deuteronomy* • Constructive Criticism • Tu B'Shevat • A Jew is Similar to a Tree • The Power of the Number Eleven • Authority Tempered with Kindness • Shevat and the Mezuzah • The Tribe of Asher • The Emblem of Asher • The Esoteric Meaning of the Letter Tzadik • Food for the Soul • The Mission of Every Jew

The Talmud asks: What is the meaning of the verse, "A man is the tree of the field?"

The response is that the "tree" refers to the Torah scholar.

-- Talmud, Tractate Taanis, p. 7A

SHEVAT

Moshe Teaches the *Book of Deuteronomy*

The eleventh month of the year is Shevat.[1] The *Book of Deuteronomy* opens by stating that Moshe explained the Torah on the first day of the eleventh month of the fortieth year from the Exodus. On this significant date, Moshe began to teach the fifth book of the Torah. He concluded on the seventh day of Adar, the same day that he passed away.[2] The beginning of *Deuteronomy* details how Moshe rebuked the Jewish people for their sins, including that of the Golden Calf, the transgressions of the spies, etc. He did not, however, specify each of their transgressions. Rashi[3] explains that in order to avoid embarrassment, Moshe *alluded* to their sins. His actions teach a great lesson: Discipline tempered with love and kindness is much more effective than stern humiliation.

Constructive Criticism

A person who is being rebuked does not find it enjoyable. He must recognize his shortcomings, and rectify his mistakes. We have to thank those who criticize us, for setting us on the right track. Moshe inspired the Jews to do Teshuva through his criticism. He used their transgressions as a guide to the future.

Tu B'Shevat

On the fifteenth day of Shevat, we celebrate Tu B'Shevat,[4] the Rosh Hashanah of trees. It is on this date that Hashem judges the trees and determines if they will be fruitful. On this holiday we thank Hashem for the wonderful fruits that he provides for us, especially the seven species from Israel.

A Jew is Similar to a Tree

The Torah[5] tells us that a Jew is compared to a tree. A tree has three sections: the roots, the trunk and branches, and the fruits containing the seeds. A Jew must always be connected with his roots, i.e. Hashem, and his Neshoma. Roots also remind us of our ancestors. The trunk and the branches symbolize our behavior and growth in Yiddishkeit. The fruits represent the joy and excitement we feel when we study Torah and perform Mitzvahs. Just as seeds are the vessel through which vegetation multiplies and ensures the continuity of the species, we must impact other Jews with similar force. We enjoy life, both physically and spiritually, and must never forget our responsibilities to our community.

Tu B'Shevat also reminds us of the Torah's position on affluence. The Torah[6] teaches that we should not forget our source, Almighty G-d Himself. The wealth that Hashem bestows upon us is to be used for a higher purpose; to educate our children, to give Tzedakah, to enhance our Mitzvahs, to buy nice Tefillin, Tallaisim, Mezzuzahs, etc.[7] The fruits are not[8] necessary for our survival; they exist for our pleasure, just as wealth does. Therefore, on the Rosh Hashanah of trees, we set our priorities upon Torah values and thank Hashem for all His wonderful gifts.

The Power of the Number Eleven

The month of Shevat is connected with the inner meaning of the number eleven,[9] which coincides with the theme of the month. The number ten represents fulfillment and completion. Eleven, however, transcends all levels of completeness. In order to reach higher levels, going beyond our limitations, we must serve Hashem with excitement. The Simcha resulting from the performance of a Mitzvah, allows us to burst forth from our mortal boundaries. Hashem then reveals his ability to transcend and blesses us, "Ad Blee Dy," meaning "I will bless you more than enough."[10]

In Kaballah we find that eleven refers to the crown of Hashem. Ten is connected with intellect and emotions. Just as a crown is placed on top of the king's head, the crown symbolizes the will and pleasure of Hashem which transcends all limitations.[11]

Authority Tempered with Kindness

The name Shevat means a branch or stick. There are many Hebrew words which describe a stick; Makel, Mateh, Aitz. The term Shaivit refers to a soft branch. It's evident why the Rabbis chose this name for this month because during this month we celebrate the Rosh Hashanah of trees. Another translation of Shevat is a royal scepter.[12] The concept of royalty is also connected to this month. A king is blessed with good fortunes and all of life's pleasures are accessible to him. Our sages[13] tell us that every Jew is a prince and deserves the riches reserved for royalty. This is demonstrated through the delicacy of the fruits eaten on the fifteenth of Shevat. Just as Moshe disciplined the Jews with love and compassion, the royal rod must be soft, *Shavit*, and not imbued with arrogance or haughtiness.[14] We are reminded to temper our authority with kindness.

Shevat and the Mezuzah

The numerical value of Shevat is 314.[15] This spells the name of Hashem, *Shadai*. This name is found on the outside of the Mezuzah, our protection from evil spirits.[16] In this month when we are blessed with an enormous amount of affluence, we need Hashem to provide us with special protection. We must be guarded from the temptation to take our good fortune for granted, or to allow ourselves to be influenced in a negative manner. It is imperative that we recognize our mission. Hashem put us here to refine and elevate the world to a higher purpose. We must assume the position of a master, and like the scepter, bestow guidance and wisdom upon our surroundings. Isaiah[17] says that the Jews must be a light unto the nations of the world.

The Tribe of Asher

The concept of elevating our pleasures to Hashem is reflected in Asher, the tribe associated with the month of Shevat.[18] The word Asher means "to praise." As it is explained in the *Targum Yonason*,[19] this tribe will be praised for their good fruits, which will be grown from their portion in the land of Israel. The word Asher, when rearranged, spells Rosh, meaning "head." When a person praises Hashem for his good fortune, and uses his wealth to spiritually impact the world, he rises to the position of the "head" of his community. A person of such stature embodies the values of a life lived according to Torah.

Asher also means good fortune.[20] A Jew who benefits from good luck must praise Hashem. Yaakov blessed his son Asher[21] with rich produce and royal delicacies. Moshe alludes to Asher's merit of providing the oil for the holy Menorah found in the Bais Hamikdash.[22]

Asher's daughter was Serach. She was instrumental in the Exodus from Egypt. As we know, the Jews promised Yosaif not to leave Egypt without transporting his body to Israel. When the Jews were preparing to leave, Moshe didn't know where to find his body. Serach showed Moshe where Yosaif was buried. She also told Yaakov that Yosaif had not been killed, but was alive in Egypt.[23] The daughters of Asher were sought by the Jewish kings and high priests.[24]

The flag of Asher was golden-yellow with a picture of an olive tree.[25] This vibrant hue symbolizes the oil with which the tribe was blessed. The oil of the olive imparts light upon the world just as Asher impacted the Jewish community with the oil at the Bais Hamikdash.

The Esoteric Meaning of the Letter Tzadik

The letter associated with Shevat is Tzadik.[26] This letter has two meanings. Tzadik means "a righteous person." In *Psalms*,[27] King Dovid says: "Tzadik Katomor Yifrach," meaning "a Tzadik blossoms like a palm tree." The palm is the king of all trees.[28] The connection between the Tzadik and the royal palm is emphasized with the celebration of Tu B' Shevat. Every Jew is righteous and has a soul that is an integral part of Hashem.[29] We all have the potential to "blossom" and impact the world.

We sometimes refer to the letter Tzadik as Tzadi, meaning "to capture." In every element of physicality there is energy. Energy is a manifestation of G-d Almighty. Hashem's energy reaches even inanimate objects. This underscores the infinite power of G-dliness. In Kaballah,[30] this energy is referred to as "holy sparks," which need to be elevated back to their source. When a Jew makes a blessing on food before eating, or when we give charity, we are redeeming the holy energy, which will otherwise be lost. We must make this world an abode for Hashem. Since every Jew possesses the status of a Tzadik, he is able to "capture," to imbue the world with Hashem's holiness.[31]

Food for the Soul

The personal attribute we must concentrate on during the month of Shevat is eating.[32] Food is a general term used to describe all of the necessities of life. It is written:[33] "Tzadik Oichel L'soiva Nafshoi," "the

Tzadik eats to satisfy his soul." This teaches us that a righteous Jew eats, i.e. pursues his physical needs, to satisfy his soul, not to satisfy his body. The physical being knows no limit, it always craves more and more. The soul yearns to elevate the holy sparks and sanctify Hashem's name through materialism.[34]

The Mission of Every Jew

The verse of the month is: "V'ihaya H'oo U'smoorasoi Y'ihiyeh Kodesh"[35] meaning that when a Jew has an animal that he is offering at the altar in the Holy Temple, that animal is holy. If he says that the holy animal shall be exchanged for another unsanctified animal, they are both holy. The concept of exchanging holiness from a sanctified being to a non-holy being is the lesson of the month of Shevat. We must elevate the mundane. As Jews, we all have the capacity to imbue the world with the message of the Torah. It is imperative that each Jew who is learned in Torah and observes Hashem's Mitzvahs, reaches out to his brothers who are less fortunate in their spiritual development and escort them home to their roots.[36] This infuses us with holiness, *Kodesh*, the final word of this verse.[37]

ADAR

The Birthday and Yahrzeit of Moses • The Lesson of Purim • Purim and Yom Kippur • The Culmination of revelation • Adar - The Powerful Mazal • Nature Is Also Imbued With G-dliness • The Tribe of Naftali • To Serve Hashem With Joy • The Wine Color and the Power of Torah • The Mystical Meaning of the Letter Kuf • The Strength of Teshuva • Laughter Verses Frivolity • Moshiach's Blessing

A Jew must begin Davening with the joy that emanates from the performance of a Mitzvah.

When a Jew experiences the joy of a Mitzvah, the Shechinah (Divine presence) reveals itself.

Talmud, B'rachos, p. 31A; Talmud, Shabbos, p. 30B

ADAR

The Birthday and Yahrzeit of Moses

The twelfth month of the year is Adar.[1] On the seventh day of this month, Moshe Rabainu was born. On the same date, 120 years later, he passed away.[2] The joyous festival of Purim falls on the fourteenth day of Adar.[3] There is a significant connection between these two events.[4]

The Talmud[5] tells us that Haman could not decide during which month he would annihilate the Jewish nation. He drew a lot from the twelve months, and Adar was selected. Haman was ecstatic since Adar contained no holidays. He also knew that Moshe had passed away during this period, an indication of decreasing Jewish Mazel. The passing of a Tzadik is akin to the destruction of the Holy Temple.[6] Haman was clever and knew how to manipulate the negative forces in order to achieve his goal of destroying the Jews. However, Haman did not know that Moshe was also born on this same date. Therefore, the negative energy that was released upon Moshe's death becomes neutralized through the positive forces surrounding the birth of our great teacher.

The Lesson of Purim

Purim means "a lottery,"[7] referring to Haman's lottery. All other Jewish holidays and festivals have Hebrew names. Purim is a Persian word. Even in the darkest moments of exile, we must never surrender. During the time of Purim, when we were surrounded by enemy nations and had no means of escape, we triumphed. *The Megillah*[8] tells us that King Achashvaroish ruled over 127 countries, most of the world at that time. The Jews were spiritually lost. Haman maintained complete control. He collaborated with the king who gave him permission to destroy the Jews.

Mordechai, the great Jewish leader, was the only one to stand up against Haman. He recognized that this holocaust was a message from Hashem which was sent to awaken the Jews from their slumber. This harsh decree was sent from G-d, through Haman and the king, as a command not to assimilate. The name "Purim" refers to the power of Almighty G-d to rescue us, even from a tyrant as wicked as Haman. At a time when the darkness stole everything from us, including Hebrew, our holy language, we still possessed the strength to transform the darkness into light.[9]

Purim and Yom Kippur

In our holy sources,[10] it is written that Purim is holier than Yom Kippur. The Torah[11] refers to the holiest day of the year as "Yom Kippurim," the Day of Atonement. Kippurim is the union of two words, Ki and Purim, when combined form the words "like Purim." We seek atonement on Yom Kippur through the act of fasting. On Purim we pursue atonement through joy and revelry. Eating and drinking become Mitzvahs. Purim underscores the Jews' remorse for their transgressions. Almighty G-d delivered us from Haman's deadly decree because we repented and reinforced our commitment to Torah. As we atone for our sins, we reveal our ability to imbue the world with holiness, even when we are having fun.

This presents a great challenge. On Yom Kippur we are like angels[12] as we transcend physicality and connect with Hashem. The challenge is to be involved with physicality *and* to elevate it to higher levels of holiness. As we reveal our strength not to lose focus during our festival meals, Hashem forgives us for our sins.

The Culmination of Revelation

The Talmud[13] tells us that Purim is the culmination of the Revelation at Mt. Sinai. Even though the Jews concluded their acceptance of the Torah at Sinai, this was only the beginning of their acceptance of G-d. Hashem placed the mountain on top of the Jews and forced them to accept the Torah. He told them that if they refused to accept it, he would bury them under the mountain. The Jews were like young children. When a child tries to run on to a busy street after he is warned of the dangers, you must limit his freedom.

The Jews were newly liberated from slavery, an oppressive existence in which they were forced to obey the dictates of masters. Upon receipt of their freedom, they were not prepared mentally to commit to the performance of the 613 Mitzvahs. Hashem commanded them to accept a life devoted to Torah. From the time of the Revelation until the time of Purim, this lifestyle was considered to have been forced upon the Jewish people. During Purim, the Jews achieved a high level of Teshuva and self-sacrifice. They were truly ready to devote their lives to Torah, and battle assimilation. This powerful experience enabled the Jews to accept the Torah not out of fear, but out of love. The festival of Purim underscores our commitment to Torah and Mitzvahs, with a renewed sense of excitement and fervor. In The Talmud,[14] it is written that on Purim, a Jew must rejoice until he transcends the limitations of his intellect and brings forth the deeper dimensions of his Neshoma and experiences G-dliness.

Adar - The Powerful Mazal

The name Adar has numerous meanings. Adar means strong, as it is written: "Adir Bamorom Hashem." During this month we experience the strength, Adir, of Hashem. Adir also means "it will endure for many generations," similar to the meaning of the word *Dor*. The Talmud[15] says that a person who seeks to sustain his properties should plant a tree called "Adir," alluding to Tzedakah, which possesses the endurance of a strong tree. The fruits of the tree are a reference to our reward of Tzedakah. The Gemara[16] says that during the month of Adar, Jewish Mazal is very potent. The Mazal of a Jew is the higher levels of his soul, which is bound with the essence of Hashem at all times. In this month we have the opportunity to draw down the Holy energy through our good deeds which are imbued with joy.

Another translation of Adar is a garment "Kiaderes Say'ar."[17] This is a reference to Hashem's compassion for His people, the Jews. The purpose of a garment is to make us look nice and feel comfortable. During Purim we experience the warmth and comfort of Hashem. A garment also serves to conceal the flesh that it covers. The miracle of Purim was concealed, it was dressed in a series of natural events. Queen Esther was Jewish and pleaded with the king to hang Haman. The king sought to please her, and hung Haman and his sons. He also allowed the Jews to defend themselves against their enemies.

Nature Is Also Imbued With G-dliness

Hashem orchestrated the great miracle that united all of these natural events. The fact that Esther became the queen was by Divine Providence. The king hosted a great feast a few years before the time of Purim. At this banquet, he became intoxicated and angry at his first queen. He put her to death, an event which laid the groundwork for the coronation of Esther.

In addition, the sequence of events which resulted in Mordechai being rewarded by the king were preordained. *The Megillah*[18] tells us that on a night that the king could not fall asleep, he summoned his servants to read to him from his diaries. They read how Mordechai had saved the king's life. The king remembered this event and was anxious to reward Mordechai. At that very moment, Haman walked into the king's chamber to ask for the kings permission to hang Mordechai. The king asked Haman what he considered a proper reward for someone whom the king wants to honor. Haman responded that the king should give that individual the royal cloak and the crown of the king should be placed upon his head. Then this person should be led through the city on the royal horses. Haman thought that the king was referring to him. He thought: "Who would the king want to reward more than me?" The king was angered that Haman would have the Chutzpah to ask for all of these honors. The king's intention was to honor Mordechai. He also realized that Haman was describing honors for himself. Haman was consequently ordered to dress Mordechai in the royal garments and escort him around the city, proclaiming Mordechai's reward.

Once again, we note how a miracle was cloaked within nature. It was Hashem, however, who placed all of the pieces together. The king could not sleep at the exact moment when Haman walked in. Haman's arrogant response was inappropriate and angered the king. These were not coincidences. They were part of a sequence devised by Almighty G-d.[19]

The word Adar is the combination of two words, Aleph and Dor, meaning "Hashem dwells."[20] Aleph refers to Hashem. He is the first, just as the Aleph is the initial letter in the alphabet. Dor means "to dwell." Hashem created the earth in order to have a dwelling place in the physical world. Through the study of Torah and the performance of Mitzvahs, we create an abode for Almighty G-d.

The Tribe of Naftali

The tribe associated with the month of Adar is Naftali.[21] Yaakov said that this tribe would be blessed with tremendous speed.[22] During Yaakov's funeral, Esau refused to bury Yaakov's body claiming that the grave site belonged to him. Naftali ran from Egypt to Israel during the burial with the deed to Yaakov's plot. Naftali's tribe was blessed with rapid produce.

Their fruit ripened quickly. Yaakov declared that Naftali should sing and praise Hashem for their fortunate lot.

To Serve Hashem With Joy

The traits associated with the tribe of Naftali, speed and singing to Hashem, are reflected in the month of Adar. The theme of the month is to serve Hashem with Simcha, joy, fervor, and enthusiasm. Simcha transcends all limitations.[23] It reveals the tremendous force within all of us. This is reflected in the traits of Naftali. We should make haste when serving Hashem. We should never procrastinate. Rashi tells us that in his blessing of Naftali, Yaakov referred to the wars between the Jews and their enemy, Sisra (during the period of the Judges). The Jews were triumphant and sang a song of praises to Hashem. Similarly on Purim, we experienced a great victory over our adversaries.

Moshe said that Naftali is rich with Hashem's blessings.[24] This is fitting as Adar, the month linked with this tribe, represents the time of the year when Jewish Mazel is overflowing. The Midrash[25] says that Naftali represents Torah. The word Naftali is similar to Nofes, meaning "dripping the sweetness of honey."[26]

Once again, we see the connection between the tribe of Naftali and the events surrounding the festival of Purim. Purim was the culmination of the Revelation at Mt. Sinai, when we committed ourselves, with tremendous spirit, to the values of Torah.

The Wine Color and The Power of Torah

The flag of Naftali was the color of diluted wine.[27] This color alludes to the study of Torah. Wine makes us feel good just as the study of Torah imbues us with a sense of well-being and makes us feel special. This hue, traditionally, is a sign of power. Torah is our strength and embodies the essence of our vitality. Naftali's symbol was a Gazelle. Yaakov said that Naftali, who is swift, is like a hind. The concept of speed is associated with joy and happiness, which can be attained through the consumption of wine.

The Mystical Meaning of the Letter Kuf

The letter associated with the month of Adar is Kuf.[28] This letter possesses several interpretations. Kuf means "to surround;" "to hit with strength," and "monkey." A monkey is a falsehood, an imitation of man. This refers to the concept of vanity. King Solomon said all is vanity,[29] this means to pursue physicality without spirituality, is foolish. To seek pleasure through materialism alone is a waste of time. The duration of this joy is short-lived. The purpose of this world is to elevate the mundane to the spiritual levels of Hashem.[30] Only spiritual pursuits are eternal. The Midrash[31] explains that a Jew who disconnects himself from a higher spiritual connection is similar to a monkey.

The Strength of Teshuva

The month of Adar reminds us of the Jew's mission in life. The Jews who lived during the time of Purim were trying to assimilate. They were involved in the consumption of non-Kosher food, ignored the laws pertaining to Shabbos, etc. They forgot their identity. They behaved like monkeys: "Monkey sees monkey does." They imitated their gentile neighbors. Hashem had to "hit" the Jews and wake them up. He sent Haman who proclaimed that the Jews are "different." The gentile recognizes the truth; we are not the same. Through Teshuva, Almighty G-d "hit" our foes with strength and "surrounded" us with his protection. The Rabbis explain[32] that the letter Kuf reflects the service of Teshuva. The left leg of this letter extends far below the line. This reminds us of the Jew who reaches a low point in his spiritual life. The power of a Jew lies in his ability to move from the depths of the lowest levels to the heights of the most elevated ones.

Laughter Versus Frivolity

The personal attribute that we concentrate on during the month of Adar is laughter.[33] Laughter is a positive act, provided that we engage in it, in a limited fashion and at the appropriate time. Our Rabbis[34] encourage us to be happy at all times, however, we must avoid frivolity. It is imperative that we integrate fun with seriousness. When we say "L'Chaim," we transcend the limitations of our Yetzer Hara.[35] As we dance and rejoice on Purim, we seek to travel to a higher plateau and unite with our essence.

Moshiach's Blessings

The verse connected with this month is "Iroi V'Lasoraikoi B'Nai Asoinoy,"[36] meaning "He will tie his donkey to the vine, to the vine branch his donkey's foal." These lines reveal a prophecy about Moshiach. When Moshiach is revealed, there will be an abundance of wine emanating from one single branch. We will then require a donkey to cart it away.[37]

The connection with Adar is evident. Purim was a breakthrough in exile. After the great miracles celebrated during this festival, the Persian rulers granted us permission to rebuild the Second Bais Hamikdash (Holy Temple). We commemorate this freedom by serving Hashem with unparalleled joy. During this period, the entire Jewish nation prays that this celebration will mark the beginning of the rebuilding of the Third Bais Hamikdash.[38]

End Notes:

Nissan **Page 1**

[1]. Parsha Bo13:4.
[2]. Talmud, Rosh Hashanah 11A; Yerushalmi, Rosh Hashanah 1: Halacha 2. [3]. Shmos Rabbah 15:12.
[4]. Rashi, Parsha V'Yairo 18:10.
[5]. Shmos Rabah 15:12.
[6]. Parsha Bo 12:41.
[7]. Parsha Pikudei 40:17.
[8]. Parsha R'eai 16:3.
[9]. Torah Oir, p. 57, side 3.
[10]. ibid. p.57, side 3; Tanya ch. 47.
[11]. Likutei Torah, p. 16, side 4; p. 17, side 1.
[12]. Parsha Lech L'Cha 17:24.
[13]. Parsha Shminee 9:24.
[14]. Likutei Levi Yitzchok Igros, p. 414. [
[15]. Likutei Torah Bamidbar, p. 11B, 12A.
[16]. B'Nei Yisasschar, p. 40 A- B Sefer Ohaiv Yisroel, p. 31.
[17]. Berachos, 4B.
[18]. ibid 57A.
[19]. B'Nei Yisasschar, p. 33 A - B; Book of Isaiah 11:9.
[20]. ibid.
[21]. Parsha Bo, ch 12:6
[22]. Parsha V'Yechee 49:8 - 12.
[23]. Parsha V'Yaishev 38:26.
[24]. Parsha V'Yaitzee 29:35.
[25]. Megilas Esther 8:16.
[26]. Talmud Sotah, p. 10B.
[27]. Talmud Brochos 13A; Shabbos 88A.
[28]. Bamidbar Rabah 2:6.
[29]. Sotah 17A.
[30]. Midrash M'Chilta Parsha B'Shalach ch. 14. End of v.22.
[31]. Rashi, Parsha V'Yichee 49:8-12.
[32]. Tanya Shaar Hayichud V'Emuna, ch. 1-12.
[33]. Parsha V'Yigash 47:23.
[34]. Parsha Lech L'Cha 17:5.
[35]. Tanya Igeres Hakodesh, ch. 5.
[36]. Parsha Breishis 2:7.
[37]. Book of Ezekiel, ch. 16.
[38]. Book of Tehillim, 51:17.
[39]. ibid. 34:13, 14.
[40]. ibid. 96:11
[41]. Talmud Rosh Hashanah, 11A.

Iyar **Page 11**

[1]. Talmud Tractate Rosh Hashana 3:A; 7:A.
[2]. Peirush Haran at the end of Tractate Pesachim; Sefer Hachinuch Mitzvahs Sefiras Haomer.
[3]. Parsha Shmos 3:12.
[4]. Talmud Rosh Hashana 11A.
[5]. Proverbs 6:23.
[6]. Parsha B'Shalach 16:1-2.
[7]. Midrash Tanchuma; Parsha B'Shalach, ch. 20.
[8]. Tehillim 40:9; Davening Maariv Prayer of "Ahavas Oilam."
[9]. Parsha B'Shalach 17:1-7.
[10]. ibid 17:8-16.

[11]. Likutei Sichos, vol. 21, p.97-99; Sefer Hayom Yom, 13th of Adar Shainy.
[12]. Rashi, Parsha Yisroi 19:2.
[13]. Parsha B'Haloischa 9:1-14.
[14]. Sefer Hayom Yom, 14th of Iyar.
[15]. Shulchan Aruch Oirach Chaim #493.
[16]. Parsha Emor 23:15-21.
[17]. Talmud Yevamos p. 62B
[18]. Sefer Pree Aitz Chaim Shar 22, ch. 7; Likutei Sichos, vol. 17, p. 505.
[19]. Zohar, vol. 3, p. 124B; Tanya Igeres Hakodesh, ch. 26; Likutei Sichos, vol. 24, p. 178-87.
[20]. Book of Kings #1 6:1.
[21]. Sefer Shaloh p. 67A; Sefer Raishis Chochma Shar H' Ahava, ch. 6; Talmud B'Rachos p. 8A. Tanya, ch. 34
[22]. Parsha B'Shalach 15:26.
[23]. Sefer Hasichos 5748, p. 410.
[24]. Bais Shmuel Shulchan Aruch Even H'Oezer #126, Sif 20, Sefer Hasichos 5751, p. 498.
[25]. Midrash Devarim Rabbah 2:14.
[26]. Sefer B'Nai Yisaschar Choidesh Iyar, p. 88B.
[27]. Parsha Kee-Sisa 34:6; Sefer B'Nai Yisaschar Choidesh Iyar, p. 87A.
[28]. Likutei Shas M'Horizal, p. 27A.
[29]. Parsha V'Yichee 49:14-15. [30]. Pirkei Avos, ch. 3, Mishnah 5.
[31]. Book of Divrei Hayomim 12:32.
[32]. Parsha V'Zois Habrocho 33:18.
[33]. Midrash Bamidbar Rabbah 2:6. [34]. Parsha V'Yaitzay 30:18.
[35]. Sefer Sichos Koidesh 5712, p. 81.
[36]. Tractate Uktzim, ch. 3, Mishnah 12.
[37]. Likutei Torah Sefer Bamidbar, p. 23, side 3; p. 33, side 4; p. 34; Likutei Sichos, vol. 22, pp. 50-51.
[38]. Likutei Shas M'Horizal, p. 27A.
[39]. Sefer Toiras Shmuel 5629, p. 314-17; Zohar, vol. 1, p. 241B.
[40]. Parsha Teruma 27:11.
[41]. Tehillim 35:10.
[42]. Zohar, vol. 3, p. 218B; Likutei Sichos, vol. 4, p. 1162.
[43]. Book of Jeremiah 9:22-23.
[44]. Parsha Breishis 4:1.
[45]. Mishnah Tractate Taanis, ch. 4, Mishnah 8.

Sivan **Page 21**

[1]. Megilas Ester 8:9.
[2]. Parsha Yisroi, ch. 19-20.
[3]. Encyclopedia Talmudis, vol. 11, p.620; Encyclopedia Oitzer Yisroel, vol. 4, p. 176.
[4]. See Rashi in Tractate Kesubos, p. 62B.
[5]. Parsha V'Eschanon 4:35.
[6]. Parsha Masay 33:11.
[7]. Parsha B'Reishis 3:20. Even Ezra on this verse.
[8]. Likutei Torah M'Horizal; Parsha Bo - Tamay Hamitzvos Kidush Hachodesh.
[9]. Reshimois "3" from the Rebbe, p. 11.
[10]. Talmud Sotah, p. 5A; Midrash Rabbah Bamidbar 13:5.
[11]. Midrash Rabbah B'Reishis 1:2.
[12]. Tanya Likutei Amarim, ch. 5.
[13]. Rashi, Parsha B'Reishis 1:1.
[14]. Talmud Shabbos, p. 88A., Rashi, Parsha V'Eschanon 6:6
[15]. Likutei Shas M'Horizal, p. 27A.

[16]. Rashi, Parsha V'Zois Habrocho 33:19.
[17]. Parsha V'Yichee 49:13.
[18]. Rashi, Parsha V'Zois Habrocho 33:18.
[19]. Midrash Bamidbar Rabbah 2:6.
[20]. Rashi, Parsha V'Zois Habrocho 33:19.
[21]. Sefer Erkei Hakinuyim M'Bal Seder Hadoirdis Erech Yam.
[22]. Tehillim 107:23.
[23]. Sefer Kesser Shem Tov, p. 19; Hoisafos #58.
[24]. Likutei Shas M'Horizal, p. 27A.
[25]. Talmud Shabbos, p. 88A.
[26]. Parsha Yisroi 19:6.
[27]. Talmud B'Rachos, p. 61B.
[28]. Rambam, Hilchos Teshuva, ch. 3, Halacha 4.
[29]. Tehillim 29:11; Midrash Shir Hashirim Rabbah 2:10.
[30]. Likutei Shas M'Horizal, p. 27A.
[31]. Tehillim 84:8.
[32]. Parsha T'Rumah 26:19-20.

Tamuz **Page 31**

[1]. Mishnah Tractate Taanis, ch. 4, Mishnah 6; Targum Yoinasan Parsha Noach ch. 8:5.
[2]. ibid.
[3]. Talmud Sanhedrin, p. 102A; Rashi, Parsha Kee-Sisa 32:34.
[4]. Book of Zecheriah 8:19.
[5]. Book of Ezekiel 8:14.
[6]. Psalms 84:12.
[7]. Likutei Sichos, vol. 18, pp. 310-17.
[8]. Song of Songs, 5:1, 6:2, 6:3.
[9]. Talmud Kidushin, p. 36A; Parsha Acharai Mois 16:16.
[10]. Parsha V'Yishlach 35:22.
[11]. Midrash Rabbah Parsha V'Yichee 88:5; Rashi, Parsha V'Yishlach 35:23.
[12]. Rashi, Parsha V'Yaishev 37:29.
[13]. Parsha V'Yaishev 37:21, 37:22.
[14]. Parsha Matois 32:1-42.
[15]. Midrash Shmois Rabbah 46:3-6.
[16]. Torah Oir, p. 45; Parsha V'Yichee.
[17]. Parsha V'Eschanon 6:4.
[18]. Rashi, Parsha V'Yaitzay 29:32.
[19]. Tanya; Likutei Amarim, ch. 44.
[20]. Midrash Bamidbar Rabbah 2:6.
[21]. Midrash Talpiyois, p. 63. Reuvain.
[22]. Parsha V'Yaitzay 30:14. Sporno.
[23]. Likutei Shas M'Horizal, p. 27A.
[24]. Book of Ovadyo 1:9.
[25]. Book of Proverbs 25:22.
[26]. Pirkei Avos, ch. 2, Mishnah 10, 11.
[27]. Parsha Yisroi 20:14.
[28]. Parsha R'ay 11:26; Likutei Sichos, vol. 4, pp. 1339-42.
[29]. Megilas Ester 5:13.
[30]. Megilas Ester 9:22.

Menachem Av **Page 39**

[1]. Mishnah Tractate Taanis, ch. 4, Mishnah 6; Likutei Sichos, vol. 23, p. 214; Sefer Get Pashut Even Hoezer #126, Sif 35.
[2]. ibid.
[3]. Talmud Sotah, p. 35A.

[4]. Likutei Torah Parsha Shlach, p. 36, side 3; Likutei Sichos, vol. 4, p. 1041.
[5]. Parsha Shlach, ch. 14; Talmud Taanis, p. 29A.
[6]. Mishnah Tractate Taanis, ch. 4, Mishnah 6.
[7]. ibid.
[8]. ibid; Mishnah 8.
[9]. Parsha Masai 33:38.
[10]. Pirkei Avos, ch 1, Mishnah 12.
[11]. Talmud Yoma, p. 9B.
[12]. Talmud Sanhedrin, p. 46A.
[13]. Likutei Sichos, vol. 23, p. 220-23.
[14]. Talmud Sanhedrin, p. 88B.
[15]. Talmud Yevamos, p. 64B, p. 65A.
[16]. Shulcan Aruch Oirach Chaim #428, #3.
[17]. Yerushalmi B'rachos, ch. 2, Halacha 4; Midrash Eicha Rabbah 1:51.
[18]. Midrash Smois Rabbah 15:30.
[19]. Torah Oir Parsha V'Yichee, p. 45B.
[20]. Likutei Shas M'Horizal, p. 27A.
[21]. Parsha V'Yaitzay 29:33.
[22]. Torah Oir, p. 45B.
[23]. Parsha V'Yishlach 34:25.
[24]. Midrash Rabbah Bamidbar 13:18; Midrash Talpiois, p. 66. Shimon
[25]. Rashi, Parsha V'Zois Habrocho 33:7.
[26]. Midrash Bamidbar Rabbah 2:6; Midrash Talpiois, p. 61. Shimon
[27]. Likutei Shas M'Horizal, p. 27A.
[28]. Midrash Alfa Baisa D'Rabee Akiva Letter Tes.
[29]. Talmud Baba Kama, p. 55A.
[30]. Parsha Breishis 1:4.
[31]. Torah Oir Parsha V"Aira, p. 55.
[32]. Likutei Shas M'Horizal, p. 27A.
[33]. Parsha V'Aira 9:3.
[34]. Midrash Tehillim, ch. 79, #3.

Elul **Page 47**

[1]. Book of Nechemia 6:15.
[2]. Rashi, Parsha Kee Sisa 33:11.
[3]. Parsha Kee Sisa 32:19.
[4]. Parsha Acharei 16:29-31.
[5]. Midrash V'yikra Rabbah 29:1. Talmud Rosh Hashono p. 11A.
[6]. Midrash Tanchuma Parsha Nasoi # 16.
[7]. Parsha Breishis 2:1.
[8]. Shabbos p. 88A.
[9]. Likutei Sichos, vol. 29, p. 272-76.
[10]. Parsha Mishpotim 21:13.
[11]. Makos p. 10A
[12]. Shir Hashirim 6:3.
[13]. Megilas Ester 9:22.
[14]. Parsha Netzsavim 30:6.
[15]. Bishalach 15:1.
[16]. Book of Michah 7:15. Likutei Sichos, vol. 22, p. 257.
[17]. Talmud Sanhedrin p. 91B.
[18]. Sidur - Rabbi Yakov Emdin.
[19]. Likutei Hashas M'Harizal p. 27A.
[20]. Parsha V'Yechi 49:19.
[21]. Parsha Matos 32:1-42.
[22]. Parsha V'Zois Habrocho 33:20-21.
[23]. Parsha Kee Sisa 32:31-32.

[24]. Talmud Shabbos p. 104A.
[25]. Parsha Bishalach 16:31.
[26]. Talmud Shabbos p. 151B.
[27]. Midrash Bamidbar Rabah 2:6.
[28]. Talmud Sotah 5A.
[29]. Midrash Alpha Baisa Drabee Akiva Letter Yud.
[30]. T'Hillim 107:8.
[31]. Likutei Hashas M'Harizal p.27A.
[32]. Talmud Sukah p. 52A.
[33]. Talmud Kidushin, p. 30B.
[34]. Parsha Bo 12:41.
[35]. Mamar Bosi Ligani 5750.
[36]. Parsha V'Eschanon 6:25.
[37]. Likutei Sichos, vol 2, p. 410.
[38]. Midrash V'Yikrah Rabbah 27:2.

Tishrei **Page 55**

[1]. Midrash V'Yikra Rabbah 29:7. Talmud Rosh Hashana 11A.
[2]. Book of Kings #1, ch. 8.
[3]. Parsha Emor 23:23.
[4]. V'yikra Rabbah 29:7 Hayom Yom 25th of Elul.
[5]. ibid 29:9.
[6]. ibid 29:7.
[7]. Likutei Torah Devorim p. 53, side 4; p. 54, side 4.
[8]. ibid.
[9]. ibid. p. 41, side 3.
[10]. Pirkei Drebee Eliezer, ch. 11.
[11]. Talmud Rosh Hashana p. 16A, p. 34B. Likutei Torah p. 51, side 2.
[12]. Mamar of Rosh Hashana Adoin Oilam 5743. Parable of the Bash't.
[13]. Parsha Emor 23:26-32. Parsha Kee Sisa 33:11 Rashi.
[14]. Zohar V'Yikra p. 73A.
[15]. Likutei Sichos, vol. 4, pp. 1149-54.
[16]. Likutei Torah B'chukoisi pp. 45-47.
[17]. Parsha Emor 23:42, 23:43.
[18]. ibid. 23:40; 23:41.
[19]. V'Yikra Rabbah 30:11.
[20]. Parsha Emor 23:36; 23:39.
[21]. Bamidbar Rabbah 21:22.
[22]. Shulchan Aruch Alter Rebbe's Hilchos Talmud Torah, ch. 2, Halacha 12.
[23]. Likutei Shas M'Horizal p. 54.
[24]. Parsha Mikeitz 42:52.
[25]. Talmud Rosh Hashana p. 11A.
[26]. Parsha V'Yichee 48:13-19 Rashi.
[27]. Parsha V'Zois Habracha 33:17.
[28]. Parsha Kee Sovoi, p. 41, side 3.
[29]. Jeremiah 31:19.
[30]. Bamidbar Rabbah 2:6.
[31]. Likutei Shas M'Horizal p. 54.
[32]. Book of Judges 3:31.
[33]. Pirkei Avos, ch. 1, Mishnah 17; chap. 3, Mishnah 10.
[34]. ibid. ch. 6, Mishnah 6.
[35]. Talmud Horiyos p. 13A.
[36]. Likutei Shas M'Horizal p. 54.
[37]. Talmud Kidushin p. 30B.
[38]. Parsha B'reishis 1:27; 1:28.

[39]. Talmud Avoda Zora p. 27A.
[40]. Parsha Lech Lecha 12:15, Chumash Heichal B'racha Komorna on this verse.
[41]. Sefer Mishnas Chasidim Mesechto Leil Rosh Hashana.

MarCheshvan **Page 65**

[1.] Tractate Tanis ch. 1 Mishnah 3.
[2.] Sefer Bnai Yisachar Month of Chesvan, p. 418.
[3.] Book of Isaiah 40:15.
[4.] Book of Kings #1 6:38 Midrash Yalkut Shimonee on this Verse.
[5.] Sefer Nachlas Shiva #4.
[6.] Rashi Parsha Matois 32:17. See Torah Oir, p. 118 A.
[7.] Shulchan Aruch Harav Oirach Chaim #114, 117.
[8.] Tractate Tanis ch. 1 Mishnah 4 ch. 3.
[9.] Parsha Eikev 11:13-21.
[10.] Talmud Sanhedrin p. 90B.
[11.] Book of Kings #1 6:38.
[12.] Torah Oir, Parsha Noach, p. 8B.
[13.] Tractate Mikvaos ch. 1 Mishnah 7.
[14.] Parsha Kee-Sisa 34:28.
[15.] Likutei Sichos, vol. 20 pp. 281-314 Parsha V'Yaitzay 32:2.
[16.] Parsha Toldos 28:5,7 Parsha V'Yaitzay 28:10-17.
[17.] Tractate Tanis p. 3A.
[18.] Parsha Breishis 2:5,6 Rashi.
[19.] Parsha Noach 8:21,22.
[20.] Tanya, Shar Hayichud V'emunah ch. 1 Teaching of the Baal Shem Tov.
[21.] Shulchan Aruch Harav #114.
[22.] Book of Izikiel ch. 16.
[23.] Likutei Sichos vol. 2 p. 545.
[24.] Parsha Mikeitz 41:50,51.
[25.] Likutei Sichos vol. 20, p. 241.
[26.] Sefer Tzemach Tzadik Parsha V'Yichee.
[27.] Midrash, Bamidbar Rabah ch. 2:6.
[28.] Baal Haturim, Parsha V'Yichee 48:19.
[29.] Rashi, Parsha V'Yichee 48:19.
[30.] Likutei Shas M'Horizal, p. 54.
[31.] Tehilim 72:17.
[32.] Talmud, Sanhedrin, p. 98B Pirkei Drebee Eliezer ch. 32.
[33.] Talmud, Zevachim, p. 113B.
[34.] Talmud, Shabos, p. 104A.
[35.] Meharal Miprag.
[36.] Talmud Brachos p.4B.
[37.] Sefer Oir Hatorah, Parsha B'Haloschah pp. 378-9.
[38.] Parsha B'haloschah 10:35,36.
[39.] Oir Hatorah Parsha Kee-Tzaitzay pp. 1025,26 Biurei Hazohar pp. 458, 59 Yahel Oir on Tehilim p. 237.
[40.] Book of Isaiah 11:9.
[41.] Likutei Shas M'Horizal p. 54.
[42.] Parsha Pinchas 28:8.
[43.] Sefer Hamamorim Milukit vol. 2 p. 248.
[44.] Parsha Kee-Savoi 26:15,16.
[45.] Book of Kings #1 12:32.
[46.] Birchas Hamazon.

Kislev **Page 73**

[1]. Tractate Mishnah Taanis ch.1 Mishnah 5.

[2]. Talmud Shabos 21b.
[3]. Darkay Moshe Tur Oirach Chaim #670.
[4]. Sefer Sharay Oira-Chanukah chs. 41,42,53 TAZ#670-Oirach Chaim #3.
[5]. Book of Proverbs 6:23.
[6]. Book of Proverbs 20:27.
[7]. Book of Isaiah 60:23.
[8]. Similar concept in Likutei Sichos vol. 1 p. 90-92.
[9]. Book of Job 8:14.
[10]. Likutei Levi Yitzchak Igros p. 223.
[11]. Sefer Bnai Yisachar Chodesh Kislev p. 43.
[12]. Midrash Yalkut Sh'monee Kings #1 ch. 6 #184.
[13]. Likutei Hashas M'horizal p. 54.
[14]. Rashi Parsha V'Yishlach 35:18.
[15]. Midrash Sifree Parsha V'zois Habrocho Pasook L'Binyanmin-Yishkoin.
[16]. Parsha V'Yichee 49:27.
[17]. Midrash Rabah Parsha Bamidbar ch. 2:6.
[18]. Sefer Oir Hatorah-Tzemach Tzedek Parsha Yisroi p. 929-30.
[19]. Book of Isaiah 11:6.
[20]. Likutei Shas M'Horizal p. 54.
[21]. Midrash Tehilim Psalm #119, Verse L'Oilam Hashem Tanya p. 152.
[22]. Midrash Oisiyois Drabee Akiva Letter "Samech".
[23]. Talmud Brachos 4b.
[24]. Likutei Shas M'horizal p.54.
[25]. Midrash Rabah Parsha B'reishis 14:11.
[26]. Parsha Bo 12:41.
[27]. Shulchan Aruch Oirach Chaim #1 Halacha 1.
[28]. Parsha V'Yichee 50:11- Rashi in Verse 10.
[29]. B'nai Yisachar Mamar Chodesh Kislev p. 41B.

Tevet **Page 81**

[1]. Megilas Ester 2:16.
[2]. Slichos for Asoro B'Teves, Siddur Tehilas Hashem, p. 356.
[3]. Talmud Sanhedrin, p. 59A.
[4]. Misechto Sofrim, ch. 1, Halacha 7; Likutei Sichos, vol. 24, p. 1-11.
[5]. Slichos for Asoro B'Teves, Siddur Tehilas Hashem, p. 356.
[6]. Book of Ezra, ch. 9, 10; Book of Nechemiah, ch. 8.
[7]. Talmud Sanhedrin, p. 21B.
[8]. Book of Ezekiel 24:2.
[9]. Avudirham Laws of Tanis Bais Yosef Oirach Chaim Simon p. 550.
[10]. Likutei Sichos, vol. 20, pp. 518-22.
[11]. Sefer Hasichos 5752, p. 237.
[12]. Parsha Emor 23:27.
[13]. Yalkut Shimoinee; Parsha B'Shalach, p. 148, #242.
[14]. Book of Ezekiel 4:3.
[15]. Rashi, Parsha Yisroi 20:22; Book of Kings #1 6:7.
[16]. Sefer Hasichos 5752, pp. 232-36.
[17]. Parsha Noach 7:8; Talmud Pesachim, p. 3A.
[18]. Mishnah Tractate Taanis, ch. 4, Mishnah 6.
[19]. Likutei Levi Yitzchok Igros, p. 251.
[20]. Book of Zechariah 2:14; Torah Oir, p. 36.
[21]. Sefer D'Var Yoim B'Yomoi, Month of Teves, p. 71B, p. 73A.
[22]. Parsha Lech L'Cha 15:15.
[23]. Talmud Baba Basra 15A; Midrash Rabbah 39:1-3.
[24]. Likutei Shas M'Horizal, p. 54.
[25]. Parsha V'Yichee 49:16-18.
[26]. Parsha B'Haloischa 10:25.

[27]. Parsha V'Zois Habracha 33:22.
[28]. Midrash Rabbah Bamidbar 2:9.
[29]. Rashi, Parsha Lech L'Cha 14:14-15.
[30]. Book of Judges, ch. 18.
[31]. Book of Kings #1 12:19.
[32]. Midrash Bamidbar Rabbah 2:6.
[33]. Parsha V'Yichee 49:17.
[34]. Likutei Sichos, vol. 11, p. 138.
[35]. Likutei Shas M'Horizal, p. 54.
[36]. Talmud Shabbos, p. 104A.
[37]. Talmud Nedarim, p. 64B.
[38]. Parsha V'Zois Ha'Bracha 33:25.
[39]. Parsha Chukas 19:17.
[40]. Tanya, p. 101; Igeres Hatshuva, ch. 12; Talmud Yuma, p. 54B.
[41]. Likutei Shas M'Horizal, p. 54.
[42]. Zohar, vol. 1, p. 27B; Rambam Hilchos Dayois, ch. 2, Halacha 3.
[43]. Tehillim 34:4.
[44]. Talmud Yuma, p. 9B; Siddur, Prayer Sim Sholom "Borchainu Avinu Kulanu K'echod."

Shevat **Page 89**

[1]. Mishnah Tractate Rosh Hashano, ch. 1, Mishnah 1.
[2]. Talmud Megilah p. 13B.
[3]. Parsha Devarim 1:1.
[4]. Mishnah Tractate Rosh Hashono, ch. 2, Mishnah 1. Sidur Bais Yakov p. 371.
[5]. Parsha Shoftim 20:19.
[6]. Parsha Hazinu 32:15.
[7]. Talmud Shabbos p.133B. Rambam conclusion of Hilchos Isurei Mizbayach.
[8]. Shulchan Aruch #207. Sefer Hasichos 5751, p. 298.
[9]. Sefer Hasichos 5752, pp. 346-51.
[10]. Sefer Malachee 3:10.
[11]. Sidur Tehilas Hashem p. 125 Posach Eliyahu.
[12]. Parsha V'Yichee 49:10.
[13]. Talmud Shabbos p. 67A.
[14]. Likutei Sichos, vol. 4, p. 1326.
[15]. Sefer Maor V'Shemesh p. 122.
[16]. Rambam Hilchos Mezuzah, ch. 5, Halacha 4. Talmud Menachos p. 33B, p. 43B.
[17]. Book of Isaiah 60:3.
[18]. Likutei Hashas M'horizal p. 54.
[19]. Parsha V'Yichee 49:20.
[20]. Parsha V'Yaitzay 30:13.
[21]. Parsha V'Yichee 49:20.
[22]. Parsha V'Zois Habrocho 33:24-25.
[23]. Talmud Sotah p. 13A. Sefer Hayashar.
[24]. Midrash Rabbah 71:13.
[25]. Midrash Rabah Bamidbar 2:6.
[26]. Likutei Hashas Mhorizal p. 54.
[27]. Tehilim ch. 92:13. Sefer Yahel OirTzemach Tzedek pp. 334-37.
[28]. Or Hasechel - Rabbi Avraham Abulafia.
[29] Isaiah 60:21. Tanya, ch. 2.
[30]. Etz Chaim 18:1. Torah Oir p. 27D. Tanya, chap. 7.
[31]. Zohar, Parsha Pinchas p. 244A.
[32]. Likutei Hashas Mhorizal p. 54.
[33]. Proverbs 13:25.

[34]. Proverbs 3:6.
[35]. Parsha B'Chukolsi 27:33.
[36]. Sefer Keser Shem Tov p. 19 - Hoisafos.
[37]. Likutei Sichos, vol. 26, pp. 90-94.

Adar **Page 97**

[1]. Megilas Ester 9:1.
[2]. Talmud Megilah p. 13:B. Tractate Kidushin p. 38:A.
[3]. Megilas Ester 9:19.
[4]. Talmud Megilah p. 13:B. Likutei Sichos vol. 16, pp. 342-51.
[5]. Talmud Megilah p. 13:B.
[6]. Talmud Rosh Hashana p. 18:B.
[7]. Megilas Ester 9:26.
[8]. Megilas Ester 1:1.
[9]. Likutei Sichos, vol. 6, pp. 189-95.
[10]. Tikunei Zohar p. 57:B. Torah Oir p. 92:4.
[11]. Parsha Emor 23:27.
[12]. Shulchan Aruch Oir Hachaim, vol. 3, Simon 610, Halacha 4.
[13]. Talmud Shabbos p. 88:A.
[14]. TalmudMegilah p. 7:B. Likutei Sichos, vol. 7, p. 26; vol. 9, p. 149, footnote 53, 54.
[15]. Baitza p. 15:B. Tehillim 93:4.
[16]. Talmud Tanis p. 29:A.
[17]. Parsha Toldois 25:25. Likutei Laivi Yitzchok Igros p. 99.
[18]. Megilas Ester 6:1-3. Talmud Megilah 15:B, 16:A.
[19]. Megilas Ester 6:5-11. Talmud Megilah 16:A. Torah Oir pp. 90-92.
[20]. Sefer Hasichos 5752 p. 399.
[21]. Likutei Hashas M'Horizal p. 54.
[22]. Parshas V'Yichee 49:21, Rashi. Midrash Rabbah Parsha Nasoi 14:23.
[23]. Talmud Megilah 7:B. Torah Oir p. 95.
[24]. Parsha V'Zois Habracha 33:23.
[25]. Midrash Rabbah Parsha Naso 14:23.
[26]. Tehillim 19:11.
[27]. Midrash Rabbah Parsha Bamidbar 2:6.
[28]. Likutei Hashas M'horizal p. 54.
[29]. Ecclesiastes 1:2.
[30]. Midrash Tanchuma Parshas Nasoi #16.
[31]. Midrash Kohelet Rabbah 1:2.
[32]. Sefer Ho'erkim Book of Letters, Letter Kuf p. 354
[33]. Likutei Hashas M'horizal p. 54 from Sefer Yetzira.
[34]. Tehillim 100:2. Torah Oir p. 20, 46:3,4.
[35]. Torah Oir p. 95.
[36]. Parsha V'Yichee 49:11.
[37]. Torah Oir p. 46.
[38]. Yerushalmi Megilah, ch. 1, Halacha 5.

The Rebbe's Torah legacy is perpetual,
his advice was most effectual,
A manhig Yisroel, unequalled,
His Ahavas Yisroel was boundless.
His inspiration will never perish,
To all who his memory cherish.

This dedication is to the revered memory of our master, teacher, and leader, Rabbi Menachem Mendel Schneerson, of blessed memory, with the hope that in his zechus, we will speedily see the dawn of our redemption.

Chana Basye and Moshe Mordechai Shuster

Mazel Tov to Eric Stein and Cynthia Fraiman on their wedding engagement, Hashem should bless them with lots of happiness and nachas.

In loving memory of my dear grandmother Hinda Frayda Bas Reb Asher Anshel Hacohen. Her spirit impacts myself and my family on a daily basis and imbues us with encouragement and excitement for Torah and mitzvahs.

Eliyahu Anshel Dalfin

In loving memory of our dear grandfather Z'ev Ben Bentzion - William Freiman O.B.M. He passed away the 12th. of Shevat, 5755. His neshoma should be bound with the eternity of life, and may he be a good beseecher on behalf of our family.

Joel and Ira Sussman

In loving memory of our dear parents and grandparents, Rebecca & Norman Sorscher, O.B.M., and Samuel & Esther Failer, O.B.M.

Dr. Raymond & Dorothy Failer
Nomi, Lisa, & Sari Failer

Mazel Tov to Nomi and Jacky Yerushalmy on the occasion of their wedding. May Hashem bless them with happiness and healthy children for many years to come.

Thank you to Rosita and Sergio Zelcer for their work in the Jewish community. May you continue to educate others by being living examples of the spirit of Judaism. You should continue to grow from strength to strength.

In everlasting memory of my beloved grandparents, Avrohom Ha-Cohen Hart, Malka Hart, Efraim Fishel ben Alexander Hoch and Gittel bas Moshe Hoch, who perished in the Holocaust. Their lives serve as an example for me to this day. May they be bound in the eternity of Hashem.

In loving memory of devoted wife, dear mother and grandmother, Celia Jonisch, Tzvia bas Shmiel, who left us on 22 Teves 5755 (December 25, 1994). She was a loving, caring, bright, and courageous lady who survived the Holocaust, raised two devoted daughters, and generations of G-d fearing Jews.

In cherished remembrance of my dear parents.
(Leon) Arye ben Avrohom HaCohen Hart,
who perished in the Holocaust. He was
a loving father and a Baal Tzedakah.
Klara Chaye bas Efraim Fishel Hart, she was a loving and nurturing mother, a messenger of Hashem who guided and protected me during the Holocaust, and later prepared me for a new life in America. She was a true Woman of Valor.
Their love and inspiration guides me through life.